Fried

Also by Joan Borysenko, Ph.D.

Books

Minding the Body, Mending the Mind

Guilt Is the Teacher, Love Is the Lesson

On Wings of Light (with Joan Drescher)

Fire in the Soul

Pocketful of Miracles

The Power of the Mind to Heal
(with Miroslav Borysenko, Ph.D.)*

A Woman's Book of Life

*7 Paths to God**

A Woman's Journey to God

*Inner Peace for Busy People**

*Inner Peace for Busy Women**

Saying Yes to Change
(with Gordon Dveirin, Ed.D.)*

Your Soul's Compass
(with Gordon Dveirin, Ed.D.)*

*It's Not the End of the World**

Audio Programs

*Reflections on a Woman's Book of Life**

A Woman's Spiritual Retreat

Menopause: Initiation into Power

*Minding the Body, Mending the Mind**

*The Beginner's Guide to Meditation**

It's Not the End of the World (five-part seminar)*

Video Programs

*Inner Peace for Busy People**

*The Power of the Mind to Heal**

Guided-Meditation CDs

*Invocation of the Angels**

*Meditations for Relaxation and Stress Reduction**

*Meditations for Self-Healing and Inner Power**

*Meditations for Courage and Compassion**

*Available from Hay House

Please visit:
Hay House USA: **www.hayhouse.com**®
Hay House Australia: **www.hayhouse.com.au**
Hay House UK: **www.hayhouse.co.uk**
Hay House South Africa: **www.hayhouse.co.za**
Hay House India: **www.hayhouse.co.in**

Fried

Why You Burn Out
and How to Revive

JOAN BORYSENKO, Ph.D.

(with her Facebook Friends)

HAY HOUSE, INC.
Carlsbad, California • New York City
London • Sydney • Johannesburg
Vancouver • Hong Kong • New Delhi

Published and distributed in the United States by: Hay House, Inc.: www
.hayhouse.com • **Published and distributed in Australia by:** Hay House
Australia Pty. Ltd.: www.hayhouse.com.au • **Published and distributed
in the United Kingdom by:** Hay House UK, Ltd.: www.hayhouse.co.uk •
Published and distributed in the Republic of South Africa by: Hay House
SA (Pty), Ltd.: www.hayhouse.co.za • **Distributed in Canada by:** Raincoast:
www.raincoast.com • **Published in India by:** Hay House Publishers India:
www.hayhouse.co.in

Editorial supervision: Jill Kramer • *Project editor:* Lisa Mitchell
Design: Jami Goddess

The anecdotes and stories submitted by Facebook friends are reprinted
here with their permission and have been edited for length and clarity. In
some of the other stories, names and identifying details have been changed
to preserve confidentiality or are composites true to the subject matter, but
not to the experience of any particular person living or dead.

The author of this book does not dispense medical advice or prescribe
the use of any technique as a form of treatment for physical, emotional,
or medical problems without the advice of a physician, either directly or
indirectly. The intent of the author is only to offer information of a general
nature to help you in your quest for emotional and spiritual well-being.
In the event you use any of the information in this book for yourself,
which is your constitutional right, the author and the publisher assume no
responsibility for your actions.

Library of Congress Cataloging-in-Publication Data

Borysenko, Joan.
  Fried : why you burn out and how to revive / Joan Borysenko, (with her
Facebook Friends). -- 1st ed.
      p. cm.
  ISBN 978-1-4019-2550-5 (hbk. : alk. paper) 1. Burn out (Psychology) 2.
Stress (Psychology) I. Title.
  BF481.B67 2011
  158.1--dc22

                                            2010030782

Hardcover ISBN: 978-1-4019-2550-5
Digital ISBN: 978-1-4019-2951-0

14 13 12 11   4 3 2 1
1st edition, January 2011

Printed in the United States of America

For my Facebook friends.
Thank you for the conversation, the
inspiration, the information, the laughter . . .
and most heartwarming of all, for your
love, prayers, and support when SkyeDancer
returned to his home in the stars.

Contents

Hell Is a
Bad Place
to Pitch a Tent

This is my 15th book, and perhaps it is the most important.

Fried may seem like an innocuous enough word since so many of us use it these days to describe our frenzied, speed-oriented, exhausted state of mind. But innocuous it is not. Feeling fried is an alarm that life has veered seriously off course. It's shorthand for losing our way individually and culturally in a world spinning so fast that it feels like we're about to be launched into outer space.

As a Harvard-trained biologist and psychologist, I've been described as a world expert on stress. However, that's not what this book is about. When you're stressed out, you keep chasing the same old carrot, whatever that may be for you. But when you're burned out, you eventually give up the chase. The hope that you can create a meaningful life fizzles out, and you find yourself sitting in the ashes of your dreams.

In a culture wedded to positive thinking, burnout and its first cousin, depression, are thought of as disorders to be fixed. But what if, borrowing a line from author and social commentator Judith Viorst, they are "necessary losses"? Perhaps they are losses of naïveté, false identities, and faulty assumptions that make way for a more authentic life.

Like many self-help authors, I write about what I need to learn. Flirting with burnout, and eventually allowing it to seduce me, is a pattern that I know all too well. When I burn out, my most loving, creative self goes missing; and I contract into a homely homunculus—the smallest, most negative version of myself. It is not a pretty picture.

I've burned out more than once—ironically, but predictably—trying to do and be my best. The pain is so great and the available help is so limited that I felt compelled to write a book that describes the inner world of burnout and how it can actually be used as a guide to inner freedom and an authentic life.

My intention is to create a map of burnout that makes the condition accessible and easily identifiable. William Styron, the Pulitzer Prize–winning author, wrote a compelling memoir of his descent into severe depression titled *Darkness Visible: A Memoir of Madness*. Psychologist Kay Redfield Jamison, a professor of psychiatry at the Johns Hopkins University School of Medicine, likewise catapulted manic-depressive illness (bipolar disorder) into full visibility in *An Unquiet Mind: A Memoir of Moods and Madness*.

While *Fried* is not a memoir in the true sense of the word, my personal experience is central to what you'll read here. Like most of my other books, this one is braided from four strands: clinical experience, psychological and biological research, personal recollections, and a larger spiritual view. Unlike any of my other books, however, *Fried* has a fifth strand—real-time input from social networking.

Sitting alone in a hotel room one night (the fate of a traveling speaker), I logged on to Facebook and asked if anyone had had experience with burnout. A landslide of responses followed. For the next year, our virtual salons deepened as one inquiry led to another and another. As many as 60 or 70 people would respond within a few hours to questions such as: *What does burnout feel like? What are its stages? Who is susceptible to it, and why? What are the physical, emotional, and spiritual aspects of feeling fried? How do you think those relate to depression? Do you have experience with antidepressants that you'd be willing to share?*

Once we had explored the anatomy of burnout together, our impromptu community turned its attention to recovering one's will and purpose, hope and wonder, faith, and the kind of "I can do it" attitude that creates what mythologist, sage, and social artist Jean Houston calls "a passion for the possible."

One evening I was thinking about the latter stages of burnout—depression and despair—and I posted this inquiry: *If you had a single sentence to share with a person in despair, what would it be?*

Facebook friend Richard Held responded with a wry one-liner: "Hell is a bad place to pitch a tent."

Richard's posting reminded me of a strange experience that occurred on the day I began writing this book. That odd happenstance turned out to foreshadow the book's structure and content.

I'd purchased a transcription program for my computer called MacSpeech Dictate, hoping that it might be more efficient to write the book by speaking it. (It wasn't.) The program does work quite well after it has learned to recognize your speech patterns, but every time I said "The Burnout Challenge," which was the working title at the time, it stubbornly typed "The Inferno Challenge" instead.

Intrigued by the computer's insistence, I spent a fascinating afternoon Googling Dante Alighieri and *The Divine Comedy,* his epic 14th-century poem. The three-part narrative is based on a series of compelling visions that Dante had during Holy Week in the year 1300, which culminated in a complete shift in his view of life. He went from feeling lost and absorbed in his own pride and apathy to feeling free and in touch with the wholeness—the holiness—of life.

In his extraordinary visions, Dante experienced a descent into the *Inferno* (the Italian word for "hell"), then a powerful self-reflective purification in the *Purgatorio* (purgatory), and a final rising up to *Paradiso* (paradise). His intention in writing this massive work was more than cataloging his experience; indeed, he was challenging his readers to make the same journey. The epic poem begins:

> *Midway upon the journey of our life*
> *I found myself within a forest dark,*
> *For the straightforward pathway had been lost.*
>
> *Ah me! how hard a thing it is to say*
> *What was this forest savage, rough, and stern,*
> *Which in the very thought renews the fear.*
>
> *So bitter is it, death is little more;*
> *But of the good to treat, which there I found,*
> *Speak will I of the other things I saw there.*
>
> *I cannot well repeat how there I entered,*
> *So full was I of slumber at the moment*
> *In which I had abandoned the true way.*[1]

When I read those opening lines, my eyes popped open and I stopped breathing for a moment. Was this written for *me?* Feeling fried—at least at its end stages—really does feel like going to hell. Getting to the point where I was working 10 or 12 hours a day for weeks or sometimes months without time off (and actually dreaming about shopkeepers and gardeners who had gentler, more spacious lives than mine) was my personal version of straying into a "forest dark." And like Dante, I couldn't really say how I had gotten so far off track. Apparently, I had fallen asleep at the wheel of my own life.

Through much of Dante's journey, he is accompanied by the poet Virgil, who leads him through the nine allegorical circles of hell, which, although unique, share one commonality: Their denizens have lost touch with the mysterious Source of Life and Love that expresses itself newly as the aliveness of each moment. They have died to possibility and are in a state of constriction and stagnation. There are a lot of ways to lose heart, but the seven deadly sins at the core of *The Divine Comedy* are a good overview: *pride, envy, wrath, sloth, avarice, gluttony,* and *lust.* These aren't just for folks who went to Catholic school. We all have plenty of experience with these excruciating states.

As my friend Wayne Muller discusses in his book *A Life of Being, Having, and Doing Enough,* it's not that these "sins" get you thrown into the fiery pit by some Divine Third Party—they *are* the fiery pit. They are love misdirected. You had hoped that they would restore you to happiness, but, in fact, they have separated you from the sweet flow of life unfolding.

In the grip of envy, for example, you miss the beauty that's right under your nose. Convinced that someone else has what you need in order to be happy, you cut yourself off from the infinite possibilities that life offers in *this* moment. Possessed by anger, you become a prisoner of the past, incapable of connecting with the gifts of the present. Tormented by greed, nothing you have is ever enough and you live with the pain of lack, unable to appreciate that life itself is a feast that has been laid out before you.

I would add another circle—another deadly sin— to Dante's allegorical description of hell: *burning out,* a state of mind in which all possibility is eventually extinguished. When you're in the latter stages of burnout, Dante's inscription over the gate of hell really hits home: "All hope abandon, ye who enter in!"

That's the bad news.

The good news is that you're free to leave the Inferno anytime you like.

The Divine Comedy, after all, is a three-part journey from hell to purgatory to heaven. In the Inferno, Dante witnesses how the various deadly sins create pain and suffering. Then, in the Purgatorio—and the root of that word means "to be purged or cleansed of"—he actively experiences how lust, rage, pride, envy, and the rest actually feel. He becomes an *active participant* in his transformation through heartfelt self-reflection. When the scales then fall from his eyes, he rises up through the spheres into paradise.

My husband, Gordon Dveirin, who has postgraduate training in literature and the history of ideas, explained to me (your basic literary ignoramus) why this mind-bending epic poem is a comedy (in classical literature, "comedy" simply means a story with a happy ending). It descends into hell, moves through the clarifying atmosphere of purgatory, and finally rises to paradise. The shape of its structure—like this book—is a smile.

Let's begin the journey by tracing the 12 stages of descent into the "Burnout Inferno." Then—just as in Dante's Purgatorio—you'll have a chance to reflect on which of your personal beliefs and behaviors have led you into the fiery pit. By the book's end—and with a little willingness on your part to examine your life—you'll begin to get glimpses of heaven on Earth.

Notes from the Underworld

"I often wonder, Joan, when we choose a book to write about (topic wise) if we are also inviting ourselves to directly experience the nature of that topic in a most intimate way. After all, how can we give pertinent wisdom if we have not ourselves experienced the journey?"

— FACEBOOK FRIEND DAVID JON PECKINPAUGH

I am hardly Dante, but I have taken several unpleasant excursions through the Inferno. The experience of being fried is not attractive, nor is it a respecter of credentials. I'm taking a risk here, revealing a side of myself that may be shocking to those of you who believe that a positive person like myself is always insanely happy. The insane part is right on—it's the happy part that's nowhere to be found when you're fried.

I'm sitting at my polished cherrywood desk completely and utterly drained. Staring listlessly out the window at the multihued foothills of the Rocky Mountains, their misty beauty is all but wasted on me.

I've deleted all the e-mails that can justifiably be trashed and some that can't, but I just don't have the juice to answer most of what's left. I pick off the easy ones first: the ones where a single sentence like "Yes, we can make it to the movies next Sunday," or "No, I can't review your manuscript" does the trick. But what about all those pesky ones that require a detailed or creative response? Forget it. They languish in the murky backwaters of cyberspace, waiting on those random moments when I temporarily return from the Land of the Living Dead.

When someone close enough to hear the truth asks, "How are you?" I compare myself to an appliance that has been unplugged. Not only can I no longer make toast, I <u>am</u> toast. My circuits are fried. Sleep is elusive; and my muscles ache, my back hurts, and I've had another string of migraines. Like Humpty Dumpty, I feel irretrievably broken. Something vital, perhaps my life force itself, seems to have gone missing. I'm emotionally exhausted and don't give a damn about work or most people. I have nothing left to give and very little interest in receiving. I just want to be left alone.

My thought process is a caricature of pessimistic cynicism worthy of an early Woody Allen film. Talk to me at your own risk because I bite. The former Queen of Compassion has morphed into the Wicked Witch of the West. Fortunately, I don't want to see anyone anyway unless it's unavoidable, which it often is since I make my living giving seminars on mind-body health and emotional wellness. What a strange absurdity.

Ah, sounds like depression, you say. Try more exercise or a smidge of Zoloft. Perhaps add some Abilify for good measure. . . .

Actually, I'm *not* in the throes of a bona fide clinical depression, either endogenous (meaning it mysteriously arises from within for no apparent reason) or exogenous (a reaction to overwhelming life circumstances). No one close to me has died recently or is even threatening to kick the bucket soon. In fact, I'm married to a loving, supportive, insightful, and fun guy. Our kids, despite being challenged by the economy, are managing well enough; our troop of beautifully parented grandkids are a delight; and substance abuse was never my thing (although I do love a glass of good red wine most evenings). And as final proof that the depression monster hasn't swallowed me whole, I can still take some pleasure in life. *I'm not dead yet.*

So What on Earth Is Wrong with Me?

Having a name for what ails you can be a relief. I remember a young mother with serious neurological symptoms who came to see me when I was running a mind-body clinic at one of the Harvard Medical School teaching hospitals. She arrived for an appointment one day unusually perky and bright. "I have MS!" she announced with enthusiasm.

She was, in fact, relieved to know what was wrong with her. Multiple sclerosis (MS) was something she could wrap her mind around—that is, she could learn more about the disease and deal with it. It wasn't a brain tumor, some previously undiscovered virus, or a mysterious alien implant. Her symptoms were the result of a known malady. Even though she knew that the course of MS was inherently uncertain and possibly uncontrollable, the devil she could name felt less dangerous than the one that had no name.

I felt the same way about whatever was ailing me. I wanted to know precisely why I felt like a zombie. Was I stressed out of my mind, overloaded with information that was jamming my gray matter and making myself so crazy-busy that I was running on empty? Had I become a poster child for Prozac, or was I simply grieving for a world that's careening out of control?

Of all people, I thought that *I* should know the answer. I'm a medical scientist and psychologist, after all. But diagnosing yourself is dangerous business. Rationalization, denial, and wishful thinking fog the lens of whatever microscope—physical, psychological, behavioral, or spiritual—you may be using to examine yourself with.

So I did the reasonable thing, which was to consult the experts. One physician—alerted by my extreme fatigue—ordered a thyroid-function test. It came up normal . . . and so did all of my blood work. In the absence of any positive physical findings, she assigned me the default diagnosis: STRESS. That was embarrassing, since it meant that I had to read my own best-selling book on the subject (*Minding the Body, Mending the Mind*). Offering me some face-saving leeway, however, she added that perhaps I was suffering from a chronic viral infection with no known treatment. I read her frustration between the lines: *Please go away. I really wish I could help, but I can't.*

So, working on the assumption that acupuncturists know more about the human energy system than physicians, I made an appointment to see one. This woman listened carefully to my history and then cocked her head, narrowed her eyes, and felt my pulses. I reclined on a massage table, and she inserted long needles in the appropriate meridians, twirling them expertly and talking to herself about my *chi*, or life-force energy. She sounded concerned.

The acupuncturist covered me with a light blanket and left for 10 or 15 minutes. After the needles were removed and I'd put my clothes back on, she came back into the treatment room with the lugubrious demeanor of a funeral director. "In 15 years of practice," she said, "I have *never* [and she leaned heavily on that word] seen someone whose life-force energy was so low." Clearly I had frightened her. So I left with a bottle of small red Chinese pills and a steely resolve never to return even if I lived out the week. The look on her face was just too depressing.

The bodyworkers I consulted were a diverse and interesting group of health-care practitioners. Massage therapists (odds-on the most pleasant variety of healers) all came to the consensus that extreme muscle tension from sitting in front of my computer, living on airplanes, and scrambling to make deadlines was the cause of my fatigue and apathy. They were spot-on about the tension, but was it the root of my profound exhaustion or just another symptom of an underlying problem?

A seasoned Rolfer (a bodyworker trained to recognize and release the tension and constriction in your *fascia,* the fibrous connective tissue that holds your muscles, bones, and organs in place) pointed out that poor posture was taking a toll on my energy. She was most helpful in raising awareness of how I sat, walked, and held my body. Rolfing sessions (ten in a series) helped stretch tight connective tissue and ease physical tension. I was grateful for the good work and reemergence of something resembling proper posture. My energy level also started to increase as I became progressively more aware of my body.

My psychotherapist, a brilliant and compassionate man whom I deeply respect, listened to my problems with great patience. We both agreed that something had to change since my life felt out of control. But short of winning the lottery and retiring to the seashore, neither one of us could imagine how my life could be improved in any practical, immediate way.

What I discovered is that burnout—outside of corporate circles—is very poorly understood. None of the healers whom I consulted—either the traditional or the complementary—understood what the mechanics of burnout are and what is needed for recovery.

I realized that unless the condition is recognized and taken seriously, physicians will keep missing it and handing out antidepressants. While medication can afford temporary relief for some people, it may also short-circuit the process of self-reflection (the important work of the Purgatorio), which is ultimately where healing comes from.

How This Book Is Set Up

I've designed this book as a journey, beginning with a guided tour of the 12 stages that make up the "Burnout Inferno." The first chapter actually comprises 12 minichapters that provide an indispensable map of the territory. You'll be able to tell exactly where you are—such as, "Yikes, I'm down at Stage 3 [putting your own needs last]. I really need to get my teeth cleaned, so, deadline or not, I'm going to make an appointment right now. Then I'm going out for a walk." In addition, each of the 12 stages culminates with a self-reflection exercise meant to help you understand more clearly why you're fried and what you need to do to revive.

Exposing and understanding the hidden patterns that lead to burnout is what the Purgatorio part of the journey is all about. You'll notice what's making you miserable and why those patterns are so strong. Then you'll be able to gradually purge yourself of the need to repeat them.

As the book progresses, you'll learn more about the personal *and* work components of burnout. You'll consider questions such as: *Are burnout and depression the same thing, or are they different animals? In what ways do adverse experiences in childhood lead to learned helplessness that increases your chances of burning out as an adult? How can you learn to manage your energy and find a dynamic state of balance? Once you pinpoint your temperament, how can you match it to the right kind of work? How do you find your passion? How do you mobilize the courage so that you can let go and move on? What is it about living in the Now that is so enlivening?*

Your trip through the Purgatorio, like Dante's, will culminate in the Paradiso. By the last chapter—"Heaven on Earth"—my hope is that you'll have a revelation of the aliveness and freedom of your authentic self.

You can enter the Burnout Inferno from a wide assortment of venues, from your home or work life or even through your spiritual life. Scales that measure burnout (the Maslach Burnout Inventory, which is the most popular) focus on three sets of symptoms: *emotional exhaustion*—deep fatigue and feelings of being emotionally drained and overwhelmed; *depersonalization*—a loss of self and a cynical disregard for the people you serve or live with; and *diminished personal accomplishment*—a progressive loss of confidence and competence.

Just because burnout hasn't made it into the lexicon of psychiatric diagnoses and treatment (the fourth edition of the *Diagnostic and Statistical Manual of Mental Disorders,* or DSM-IV, is the bible of the craft) doesn't make it any less real. If burnout ever does make it into the DSM, we'll all know about it in a heartbeat. It will become the syndrome du jour—the last, best hope of Big Pharma (the gigantic pharmaceutical industry that invents extremely lucrative drugs for everything from cancer to restless legs syndrome to growing thicker eyelashes).

Burnout is a natural for Big Pharma. Imagine commercials for drugs that promise to rekindle your inner fire, conquer fatigue, or power your motivational engine. They could dominate the ad world.

They already have, in fact. They're just called antidepressants. One of the reasons multiple studies have shown that antidepressants are no better than placebos (except in very severe cases, as you'll read about a bit later) is because they're prescribed largely to people who aren't really depressed. These individuals are in the process of burnout, which *includes* a component of depression, but can only be ameliorated by understanding the mechanics of the process and changing one's orientation to life and work.

With a Little Help from My Friends

The research on burnout comes alive through the comments of my Facebook friends (from now on, I'll abbreviate *Facebook friend* as FBF), which are laced through every chapter. Thanks to their contribution, the research findings (fascinating though they are) are grounded in a diversity of human experience.

Here's a little background info: 75 percent of my Facebook community is female, and 25 percent is male. The age range is predominantly from the mid-40s to what Facebook calls 55+, although 20 percent of my friends are between 25 and 45 years old. They are teachers, doctors, nurses, psychologists, students, corporate executives, parents, grandparents, folks who are out of work, and retirees. Every time I've asked them for support—either personal or professional—they have been there for me. I am both touched and very grateful.

Early on, a remarkable woman by the name of Beverly Potter joined the burnout conversation. Beverly has been writing books on burnout since 1980—not long after the syndrome was first named. A behavioral psychologist, corporate consultant, and author, she dropped into the conversations like a fairy godmother. One day as I sat contemplating how to organize this book and what the best contribution I could make might be, she sent me this message:

In researching burnout, you've probably noticed that a lot of the "literature" is stress repackaged as burnout, making the two interchangeable, murky concepts. Burnout is not stress or caused by stress. It results from "learned helplessness"—and is stressful. The stress must be managed, but managing stress does not deal with the burnout.

Burnout is a motivational problem. The victim can't get going. It affects focus and stick-to-itiveness. It is also an existential crisis—a spiritual "emergency." The person becomes enveloped in a "Why bother?" attitude: in despair, in settling, in depression, in giving up. Many animals in learned helplessness experiments inexplicably died. They just gave up.

Within a spiritual context, how does one deal with helplessness? With despair due to the futility of the endeavor? How does one self-empower? These are difficult questions, and there are no quick fixes. It becomes more of a lifelong discipline of becoming. How one handles the spiritual challenges of burnout is an area where you could make a significant contribution—an area that has largely been ignored.

Here goes, Beverly. With a little help from our mutual Facebook friends (the FBFs), I've set out to do exactly what you suggested.

Chapter One

Mapping the Descent into the Inferno

"Sometimes we need permission to surrender to the feelings of burnout in order to take stock, be gentle with ourselves, and begin to safely rebuild our lives. Too many people these days keep powering through, toughing it out, until they collapse. They don't feel that they have permission to stop and put themselves first."

— FACEBOOK FRIEND JAN CARMICHAEL DAVIES[1]

I wrote a first-person account of burnout in the Introduction to give you a taste of how it affects thinking, behavior, emotional experiences, relationships, and work in the world. But unless you've experienced burnout personally, you may not fully comprehend how serious this state of emotional exhaustion and loss of motivation can be, and how crucial it is to meet its challenge before you collapse into depression, addiction, or physical illness.

One of my FBFs kicked off an interesting conversation by commenting on how defensive she got when a friend told her that she was fried and that her lifestyle simply wasn't sustainable. Another FBF concurred, adding that she used to think that being burned out was an admission that something was wrong with her. Now she views burnout as an invitation to come into alignment with a more elegant expression of her gifts, relationships, and overall life energy.

The late psychologist Herbert Freudenberger, who first popularized the condition in his 1980 book, *Burnout: The High Cost of High Achievement*, would have appreciated their conversation. Rather than a cause for shame, Freudenberger believed, burnout is a painful affliction of good people who are trying to give their very best. He defined it as "the extinction of motivation or incentive, especially where one's devotion to a cause or relationship fails to produce the desired results."[2]

Freudenberger and his colleague Gail North distinguished 12 stages as a general map of the territory that leaves plenty of room for individual variation. Some people endure all or most of the stages of burnout, and others experience just a few. Some go through them chronologically, while for others, they are simultaneous or occur out of order. From my own experience, both personal and clinical, the 12 stages of burnout are powerfully descriptive of the thoughts, feelings, and actions that define the syndrome.

The observations that Freudenberger made, drawn from extensive interviews, laid the foundation for the research that followed.[3] He traced the progression of burnout from the first phase of wanting to prove yourself and do a good job to an escalating set of emotional, behavioral, and physical symptoms that accompany the realization that doing a good job according to your own definition or that of others is virtually impossible. Falling short of your ideal in any way—perceiving a gap between what you think is required of you and the reality of what you can produce—can be disheartening to the point where your entire sense of self crumbles.

The reality gap can open in a variety of ways: for example, the kind minister who finds himself under attack from a few troublemakers in the congregation who are impossible to please; the physician who is overworked and unable to practice the kind of medicine she signed up for; the social worker unable to handle her caseload and help her clients move forward in their lives; the eager worker unclear about his job description; the ecologist incensed when political horse trading kills off environmental initiatives; the hardworking parent whose child turns to drugs; and the list goes on. . . .

While I've stayed true to the stages of burnout that Freudenberger and North originally described, I've changed some of their names so they're more descriptive. I've also added my own unique spiritual perspective. Since it's so important to understand the patterns that propel the journey into the Burnout Inferno, this lengthy chapter is best approached as 12 minichapters. Take your time reading through each of the stages. When you're finished, please read through them a second time; and then at your own pace, complete the "Self-Reflection Exercise" at the end of each stage, which is at the heart of your revival. Here's a quick breakdown of the burnout stages:

Stage 1:	Driven by an Ideal
Stage 2:	Working Like a Maniac
Stage 3:	Putting Your Own Needs Last
Stage 4:	Miserable, and Clueless as to Why
Stage 5:	The Death of Values
Stage 6:	Frustrated, Aggressive, and Cynical

Stage 1: Driven by an Ideal

Freudenberger characterized this stage as a compulsion to prove oneself.

I know the feeling. The year was 1981, and it was as busy a time as I can remember. My husband of that era (Miroslav, who is still a good friend) and I both commuted an hour or more each way to work. He was doing research in comparative immunology and teaching medical students at the Tufts University School of Medicine in Boston. I was doing research in human motivation and health with Harvard psychologist David McClelland. I was also studying for the licensing examination as a clinical psychologist and planning to open one of the country's first mind-body clinics with cardiologist Herbert Benson at Boston's Beth Israel Hospital.

We lived in a small rural community, focused on giving our young sons, Justin and Andrei, a healthy outdoor life. All of us tended the vegetable garden in the summer and solar greenhouse in the winter. In addition, a barnyard full of chickens, ducks, geese, pheasants, king pigeons, guinea hens, and peacocks required our considerable time and attention year round, as did our two horses. Then there was my elderly mother. If I missed our evening phone call, the next night I'd be met with steely silence followed by a comment like, "Oh, I thought you were dead." She meant to be funny, but burned-out people quickly lose their sense of humor.

I was fiercely committed to my children, marriage, and the new field of behavioral and integrative medicine. Furthermore, I was at the stage when I still believed that it was possible to reach enlightenment *now*, in this very lifetime, if you meditated long enough and did sufficient amounts of yoga. But I just couldn't pull it all off.

The kids hated that I was a working mom and told me so loudly and frequently. They would have gladly traded our nice house and all the animals for sitting at home with me in an egg-stained nightgown instead of being dropped off at day care to wait for the school bus. My marriage was faltering, my mother thought I was nuts, and I realized that a life of grant writing and research was not what I'd signed up for.

My relief valve? I ran at least 20 miles a week, and for every mile I ran, I allowed myself one cigarette. This was done on the sly . . . behind a tree or the garage, or in a parking lot on the way home from work. I sneaked those smokes wherever I could to numb the pain of burnout—of falling into the gap between the world I so much wanted and the reality of the world I lived in.

The FBFs, like Freudenberger, made note of the fact that people who have the greatest investment in projects and ideas are much likelier to burn out than those who are less attached to the outcome of whatever they're involved in. Although commitment to a cause, a job, or your children may seem selfless and virtuous, there's often an underlying ambition and motivation to prove your importance and worth that predisposes you to becoming fried.

Motivation is a complex and largely unconscious orientation to what we do and how we do it. Do we "do" from a sense of insufficiency, just to prove that we deserve to breathe air and take up space? Do we do to make a living, plodding along like an automaton? Do we like what we do, but do more than we'd like so that we can feed our family? Do we do out of guilt or penance, trying to be good? Or perhaps we are so fervent about our efforts simply because we feel called by a power that cannot be denied.

Sometimes it's the passionate doers—those out to save the world or to save souls—who are the most prone to burnout. The late Trappist monk Thomas Merton wrote a famous letter to a young activist named Jim that addressed just this point. In it, Merton wrote the following:

> You are probably striving to build yourself an identity in your work and your witness. You are using it, so to speak, to protect yourself against nothingness, annihilation. That is not the right use of your work. All the good that you will do will come not from you but from the fact that you have allowed yourself, in the obedience of faith, to be used by God's love. Think of this more and gradually you will be free from the need to prove yourself, and you can be more open to the power that will work through you without your knowing it.[4]

Whether or not you relate to the religious context in which Merton wrote, he made a point that I resonate with deeply. The more attached I get to a particular outcome, the less that Life can flow through me. More often than not, synchronicity opens doors that I would have

6

never imagined. But if I'm wedded to my own agenda, I'm likely to walk right past those doors without even noticing them.

It gets exhausting when you believe that you're personally responsible for changing the world. Here is more advice from Merton as he advised the young man:

> Do not depend on the hope of results. When you are doing the sort of work you have taken on, essentially an apostolic work, you may have to face the fact that your work will be apparently worthless and even achieve no result at all, if not perhaps results opposite to what you expect. As you get used to this idea you start more and more to concentrate not on the results but on the value, the rightness, the truth of the work itself.[5]

Self-Reflection Exercise #1:
What Motivates Your Work?

First thing in the morning (for me, that's after a cup of coffee!), pull out a notebook and pen. The unconscious is a natural neo-Luddite that expresses itself most authentically in longhand. The writing exercises I'll describe in this chapter work best if you keep the pen moving on the paper and don't stop to read or edit what you've written. This stream-of-consciousness approach taps into your authentic self, the part of you that is directly connected to the larger intelligence that Merton calls God—the primal energy of creativity.

Write for at least 30 minutes about what motivates your work in the world. Chances are those motivations are complex.

When I think about what motivates my mothering, for example, it's partly biological, partly narcissistic in that I want my children to reflect well on me, and partly (and I like to tell myself that this is the biggest part) that I want my children to develop fully into their own selves so that they enjoy their lives and leave the world a little bit better than they found it. I also hope that they'll be there for me if I'm fortunate enough to make it to old age. These are just a few of the layers of mother motivation that came directly to mind.

You can do this inquiry on motivation with any or all of your relationships. Next, try it with your work. For me, being a scientist, psychologist, author, and public speaker is its own mixed motivational bag. When I get attached to results (that this book makes *The New York Times* bestsellers list, for instance), I'm setting myself up for burnout. But if I can be content to "concentrate not on the results but on the value, the rightness, the truth of the work itself," as Merton suggested, then there's nothing to prove. There's only a gift to be given.

What comes to you during this exercise is the starting point for transforming burnout to insight, and freeing your best self for work and for life.

Stage 2: Working Like a Maniac

This is the stage that Freudenberger described as "working harder" so that you can move closer to your goal. Most of us work harder on some occasions than at others, of course. I'm always relieved when our accountant, for instance—who seems to hyperventilate through the entire six-week run-up to April 15—relaxes at the end of another tax season. When I was in the business of conducting research on stress, accountants at tax time were often recruited as naturally occurring experimental subjects.

But there is no "high season" if you're sliding down into the Burnout Inferno. Every day is busy and filled with stress when you're intent on proving yourself.

Meticulous about your work, you may be unwilling to risk delegating anything you consider important so that other people can help you carry the load. A kind of grim determination takes over, a "do or die" attitude that leads to taking on more than can be realistically accomplished. In these days of budget reductions and downsizing, even individuals who aren't motivated by idealism but just want to do their jobs reasonably well are feeling the squeeze. Many of the FBFs wrote about being assigned more work than was humanly possible to accomplish after colleagues were laid off. They admitted to being overly stressed out.

When I was working with Dr. Herbert Benson, he introduced me to the Yerkes-Dodson law, which makes the relationship between stress and burnout clear. Visualize a graph. Succinctly put, if you place productivity on the y-axis (the vertical line) of your graph and stress on the x-axis (horizontal line), you get an inverted *U*. Productivity increases with stress—*to a point.* But after that point, you find yourself in the land of diminishing returns. You're working harder, but getting less quality work done. That's when burnout sets in.

Here's an example: The stress of working toward a deadline—whether it's cleaning your house before company comes over or finishing a demanding work project—can be exciting and energizing. Intention focuses attention, and when the challenge of the assignment and your degree of mastery intersect optimally, the exhilarating state that psychologist Mihály Csíkszentmihályi calls *flow* takes over and you're golden.

Flow occurs around the peak of the Yerkes-Dodson curve. But if the deadline you're working toward is unrealistic, or if your level of mastery isn't sufficient to meet the challenge, then you slide off the peak of the curve and down the descending limb. You're working harder, but the quality of what you do isn't your best. Your mental health isn't that stellar, either.

Likewise, when you're hovering near the edge, unforeseen problems (such as a fight with your spouse, your kids doing poorly in school, an illness, a tax problem, a death in the family, or even a new software program that you're expected to start using at work) can push you into the abyss.

When I ran a stress-disorders clinic, I saw a lot of people who were very productive—including a lot of high-powered executives—even though they were stressed out and working on the burnout side of the curve.

By learning to back off and pay attention to their own needs, however, many of these individuals were able to bring a different, more balanced and mindful self to the office. Their leadership skills became more open and responsive as they moved back over to the ascending limb of the curve. Not only did their work still get done, but the quality of it was of a different caliber—more innovative, exciting, and evocative both of their talents and those of the people they worked with.

Moments of astounding flashes of creativity are filled with examples of breakthroughs that came by working *less*. The French mathematician and physicist Jules Henri Poincaré, for example, experienced a major insight on a difficult formula while on vacation in the French countryside. We can all take a lesson from the science of creativity. Inspiration does indeed favor the prepared mind, but the Muse is courted by Lady Pleasure and scared off by cracking the whip.

If you take time out, amazingly enough, the world actually keeps spinning in its orbit, and you'll do a better job. You'll also protect your adrenal glands from burning out along with your own creative spark.

When I was doing research at Harvard, the head of the Sufi Healing Order came to Boston. I attended a weekend retreat with him to see what this ancient mystical school (the poet Rumi was a Sufi) might teach us about healing. Saul the Sufi healer affirmed that there are two very different ways to approach healing and life: powering through by pressing your own agenda, or relaxing into a larger source of energy that carries you along.

While walking along the beach with Saul, discussing whether or not healing energy could be measured in a laboratory, the conversation got personal. He could tell I was pushing so hard that my adrenal glands were working overtime. Why not back off and let universal energy come through me, he suggested, rather than manufacturing a more limited energy on my own and wringing my adrenal glands dry?

Why not, indeed? Prevention of burnout begins with becoming more mindful of your own physical energy system.

Self-Reflection Exercise #2:
Minding the Energy Body

Your body is the most obvious place to begin shifting your relationship to energy. Right now, for example, I'm relaxed. A hike up the mountain with Gordie and the dogs, a hot shower, and meditation make for mellow. If I were to rate my stress level (1 being low and 10 being high), it would be a 3 at this moment. My body feels relaxed, open, and in balance. But, of course, that's not always the case. If I didn't know what 10 felt like, this book wouldn't be of much use to you.

The key is not to reach for Level 1 and stay there, but to become a connoisseur of your changing physical sensations, which can then guide you. When I'm at a 7 or 8 on a 10-point stress scale, for example, I know that I'd better take a walk, relax, play with the dogs, or call a friend since I can't focus well. Flow, that delightful state when your best work happens, occurs near the midpoint of the Yerkes-Dodson curve.

My colleague and friend Shannon Kennedy (also an FBF) is a Feldenkrais practitioner who has a lot to say about burnout and the body. Feldenkrais is a form of bodywork that enhances awareness of how you hold yourself and how the aliveness within you—your energy body—waxes and wanes responding to mental, emotional, and physical stimuli.

Shannon posted this during one of our discussions:

> The body is where I would start to deal with burnout so that I wouldn't need to take long sabbaticals to collect my parts and return them to their original location. So often we intellectualize

and go to the mind to think things through, jumping right past the physical discussion our body is having right under our nose. My perspective is this: getting to know where you feel contracted in body, thought, and emotions *and* what it feels like to release that holding is the way out of burnout.

We are fluid, flowing beings, and when we are in nonstop mode, we are perpetually in a holding contraction, thinking that we are stabilizing. Our body is actually working overtime to support our mind's directives, like a loyal canine companion. Because of this contraction, no blood/prana can flow.

When I ran a mind-body clinic, body awareness was one of the first skills we taught our patients. Simple progressive muscle relaxation—tensing and relaxing your body methodically, part by part, from head to toe—trains you how to notice muscle tension and its relation to energetic vitality (what Shannon referred to as *prana*).

Whether you purchase a guided muscle-relaxation CD (try my *Meditations for Relaxation and Stress Reduction*) or sign up for Feldenkrais lessons or mindfulness, tai chi, or yoga classes, these disciplines train body awareness. In a matter of weeks, you'll become a budding connoisseur of subtle body sensations.

Here's one thing you're sure to notice. When you get into the mental mode of needing to achieve and to prove yourself, pressing an agenda and squeezing your adrenals, you'll tense up and cut off the flow of prana and creativity. When you let go, you'll automatically relax and gain access to your inner wisdom. Taking care of yourself is the most important part of taking care of business.

Stage 3: Putting Your Own Needs Last

FBF Jeanette Pintar posted this comment that describes what happens when you're constantly putting your own needs last:

> But how can I take care of myself when *I must* get all this stuff done?! That's my first clue that I'm burning out . . . that and all the lightbulbs around me start to burn out! Defensive? Offensive? Just plain whiney and cranky? Those are good clues, too.
>
> I have to remind myself to step away from the computer, step away from the to-do list, put the guilt trip down, and ditch the martyr syndrome. I take a salt bath, walk the trails, or go to the beach. I at least go out for a cup of coffee or drinking chocolate and take a few minutes to reset. The irony is that in taking more time for me, I seem to get everything else done with more grace, ease, passion, creativity, energy, and enthusiasm in much less time than before.

Jeanette is doing well because she has learned to catch herself in the act of putting her own needs last. If you don't catch yourself, this is the stage of burnout where your physical body and mental health begin to quickly lose ground because you're too busy to tend to your well-being.

Good-bye exercise, hello belly fat. Good-bye movies and walks in nature that provide relaxation, enjoyment, and the shift to right-brain thinking that favors creative breakthrough and conscious contact with a larger source of intelligence. Good-bye time with family and friends. You exhaust yourself in doing, doing, doing. Thus the popular saying: "Put on your own oxygen mask before helping anyone else." That advice, however, makes me see red when I'm "initialized" (taken over by relentless deadlines and working myself into a frenzy). It interrupts my need to achieve and creates anxiety, which I instantly convert into irritation.

This is when one of my girlfriends—I'll call her Gayle—reliably starts calling me a "human doing." That phrase, like the oxygen-mask metaphor, annoys me to no end. (And since I'm generally a kind, easygoing person, being annoyed is another surefire indication that I'm burning out.) I get defensive. I compare myself to much busier people—Hillary Clinton comes directly to mind—who are so enthusiastic about what they do that the term *fried* apparently doesn't apply to them, at least in my imagination. If you asked her (or Bill), perhaps they'd tell you a different story. But I use Hillary and other apparently indefatigable role models as an excuse nonetheless.

On the other hand, what if someone had accused Benjamin Franklin of being a human doing on the verge of burnout, for example? Just as he was gearing up to fly his kite in a thunderstorm and discover electricity, my friend Gayle might have said, "Relax, Ben, before your blood pressure goes through the roof. You work too hard. Just look at those bags under your eyes and that enormous paunch! You need more exercise and sleep. You have to take better care of yourself. Maybe you could learn to meditate and reduce your stress."

My fantasy is that Franklin might have rolled his eyes, patted his ample girth, and laughed until he cried. Then, perhaps, he might have grabbed Gayle by the hand and taken off running into the storm. Enthusiasm, of course, *is* an antidote to burnout. It's medicine for the soul—the place of flow where doing and being are one. And although I might wish that Hillary Clinton had more time for herself, she'll likely outlive us all because so much life-force energy moves through her.

The etymology of the word *enthusiasm* can be traced to the Greek root *entheos*, which means "in God"—inhabited and guided by the life force itself. The operative question to ask when *you* aren't taking time for yourself is whether you're inspired like Benjamin Franklin or Hillary Clinton; or emotionally drained, overdriven, and exhausted. To avoid lying to yourself and getting defensive (which you can already appreciate is typical of burnout), you can pose the question in another way: *Am I having fun and enjoying life?*

Self-Reflection Exercise #3:
Are You Having Fun Yet?

On a scale of 1 to 10 where 1 is feeling like Ebenezer Scrooge on a bad day and 10 is like Robin Williams, what's your joy-in-life score? Write it down, because you'll need to return to it later to see how your revival is coming.

One evening while writing this book, I was a guest on the Inspiring Women Summit, a teleseminar conference. The other two guests were my colleague Christiane

Northrup, M.D., an obstetrician-gynecologist whose current work in women's health is all about pleasure; and her teacher of pleasure, the inimitable Mama Gena (Regena Thomashauer) who runs the renowned Mama Gena's School for Womanly Arts in New York City.

"What are you wearing?" Mama Gena asked us. *She* was wearing a feather boa, lace teddy, and something silky and slippery around her loins. Seated amidst multiple glowing candles, Mama Gena was certainly practicing what she preaches and apparently having a lot of fun. Christiane reported that she was wearing tango shoes with four-inch-high red heels. I, on the other hand, was completely resplendent in my droopy sweats while sitting at the computer.

We had a wild time. When I wasn't editing my language for posterity (the series was recorded), it was actually great fun, although I realized what a prude I am. I was actually holding my breath while Christiane and Mama Gena waxed ecstatic about that tiny marvel of feminine anatomy—the clitoris—and its 8,000 pleasure-happy nerve endings.

"How does it feel down there?" the two Pleasure Mavens inquired. "Is your pelvic floor feeling alive?" Although I sat blushing in my less-than-sexy sweats, it was impossible to avoid taking stock of the state of those 8,000 nerve endings. I understood their point perfectly well. The organs of reproduction (no matter which sex you belong to) are the seat of your life-force energy. If things are dead down there, it's a signal that you're running out of gas in the rest of your body *and* your life.

Mama Gena offered this advice: You don't revive from burnout by thinking about it and dissecting your problems. You have to wake up through pleasure and fun. Joy makes you more enthusiastic about life. And as Dr. Northrup pointed out, pleasure increases the amount of nitric oxide in your blood, which enhances cardiovascular health and general well-being.

So . . . tango, anyone? What fun are *you* looking forward to? Try scheduling one pleasurable activity every week for the next three months. Put those dance lessons, hikes, camping trips, romantic dinners, evenings out with the girls or guys or couples, or whatever you can dream up on your calendar. Even if (especially if) you don't want to follow through, make the effort, and then at the end of three months, go back and revisit your fun score. If it hasn't changed, you may have to visit Mama Gena's School for the Womanly Arts or whatever the masculine equivalent may be.

Stage 4: Miserable, and Clueless as to Why

FBF Laurie Line didn't even realize that she was burned out until losing her job gave her the time to take a breath and notice what she was actually feeling. Here's how she described the experience:

> When my burnout became apparent after being laid off, I was finally able to slow down and realize that I had been selling my soul for unending deadlines and always being the go-to person for everyone else's needs. In the middle of it, I believed that things would get better after the deadline, after I crossed something off my list, and so on. However, the universe knew that the only way for me to see clearly was to have a long break away from the craziness.

A friend of mine who is an obstetrician was as clueless as Laurie about why she was so out of sorts. To compound the problem, "Jenna" did what a lot of stressed-out people do: she looked for someone else to blame for her feelings. It must be her husband! "Steve" could be more attentive when she came home from work and more intimate before bed (and while in it). He could take up more of the slack around the house, too. After all, wasn't he supposed to be her other half, her soul mate who would make everything right with the world? Obviously, Steve was shirking his marital responsibilities. But her husband *wasn't* the problem; it was Jenna's burnout that was talking, rather than her good heart.

Like many couples, Jenna and Steve had some wrinkles to iron out, but from Steve's point of view, his wife's constant fatigue and defensiveness made it hard to be intimate. He felt that she just wasn't the same energetic, fun-loving woman he'd married. Moody, touchy, and exhausted, Jenna was difficult to be around because she was consistently negative.

The underlying reason for Jenna's burnout was a double bind—a "damned if you do, damned if you don't" kind of work situation. She loved being an ob-gyn and had put off having children of her own in order to give other women safe passage through pregnancy and birth. Jenna's clientele consisted of high-need, high-risk cases—women who were experiencing the stress of infertility as well as those who were at risk of not being able to carry their babies to term.

Jenna loved these women as if they were her own family. She was dedicated to long appointments so that she could inform, reassure, and motivate her patients to do whatever might be necessary to ensure a healthy pregnancy. How could she allot 15 minutes to a woman who'd recently lost a baby at four or five months' gestation? But as the cost of her malpractice premiums rose, she was forced to schedule more patients for shorter visits just to make ends meet financially. Eventually, the strain of being pulled between taking good care of her patients and attending to her own needs became unbearable.

With the help of her husband and a therapist, Jenna finally made the difficult decision to leave her practice and take six months to rest and reflect on her life. As I write this, she's nearing the end of her sabbatical and planning to take a part-time job at a Planned Parenthood clinic. She'll still be able to care for women who need her but without the stress of the high-stakes, high-risk practice she'd been in before.

Self-Reflection Exercise #4:
What's Going On in Your Life?

If you're feeling frustrated, aggravated, or disempowered, and if you catch yourself always blaming other people for your problems or complaining about their performance, you need to connect with what is really going on. *Is it them, is it a situation that requires a change, or is it you?* You need a real time-out to evaluate your life, even if it's not a six-month sabbatical like Jenna's.

Taking the time to sort through what you're feeling is hard to do in familiar surroundings when you're moving at the speed of light, out of touch with your body and emotions. The ringing phone, ceaseless e-mails, household chores, work issues, and all your relationships are distractions. Fortunately, you can visit what are aptly called "retreat centers" all over the country. Since I often give workshops at such places, I've sampled the spectrum from five-star spas to two-star retirement communities for nuns who rent out rooms to the public.

When I lived on the East Coast, and had just left my job at the hospital after being in a head-on collision (which was due to burnout), I went to several weekend retreats at a Benedictine monastery about ten minutes down the road from my house. There was no program; it was simply a place of refuge at a price less costly than feeding myself at home. The accommodations were spartan but clean, and I was alone—no kids, no husband, no business to conduct. Jesus was there, of course—at least in spirit—but he and I did our own thing.

I'm Jewish by birth and spiritual but not religious, yet that retreat was perfect for me. I was free to explore the beautiful trails, and was fed three meals a day. My room was pleasant and a good place to meditate, journal, or just read a mystery novel and relax. Furthermore, I didn't have to talk to anyone unless I wanted to.

Both of the Canyon Ranch sites (beautiful spas located in Lenox, Massachusetts, and Tucson, Arizona) are oases with access to nature, healthful food, state-of-the-art wellness and exercise programs; and practitioners such as physicians, bodyworkers, exercise physiologists, psychologists, and spiritual mentors. Less-expensive retreat centers that offer excellent programs are the Kripalu Center for Yoga & Health in Stockbridge, Massachusetts; the Omega Institute in Rhinebeck, New York; the venerable Esalen Institute in Big Sur, California; and my all-time favorite place on the planet—the Hollyhock retreat center on beautiful Cortes Island, British Columbia. Several of these places also offer work-study programs. Over the years, I've met some very interesting people—from corporate executives to health-care providers, students, and homemakers—who were taking a break from their lives by affording themselves these types of opportunities.

If you search the Internet, you'll almost surely be able to find a retreat center that fits your budget. Take out your calendar and make those plans now. Otherwise, your busy life will just keep rolling along until you finally crash emotionally or physically . . . or, like I once did, quite literally.

Stage 5: The Death of Values

My friend Tom Zender is a minister, author, and business consultant with very strong values. One reason why he doesn't burn out is reflected in a comment he made on my Facebook page. It was in response to a discussion on how getting sick is often the only way in which busy people can get a rest. Tom wrote: "We've got to block out at least an hour per day for meditation, silence, prayer, reading, journaling, exercise, communication with family and friends . . . er, make that *two* hours, Joan!"

Well, I know that all of those things are important, and I not only subscribe to them, I teach them. But when burnout takes over, values get shoved aside so that you can spend every minute working. Priorities shift from living a balanced life to chasing an unobtainable moving target. A good example of this is in the movie *Avatar,* where a degenerate culture (which was modeled on our own) was willing to destroy a peaceful planet (which was in tune with the natural world) in order to excavate a mineral aptly named *unobtanium.* The metaphor wasn't lost on me, nor was it lost on the millions of others inspired by this mythical film.

When you're single-mindedly chasing after your own unobtanium, you eventually flatline—effectively becoming deadened to the richness of life unfolding all around and within you. The little blips of joy, relaxation, fun, and spiritual refreshment that give meaning and texture to life disappear. When I've been in this state, nothing seems to matter anymore. I don't care about going to the movies, seeing family and friends, exercising, getting a massage, gardening, or even talking back to the hypocritical politicians (the ones who tout family values while cavorting with their mistresses or bash homosexuals while having same-sex lovers) who populate the television news. Now that's a dire symptom. It's as if all of my interests and pleasure receptors have dried up and fallen off.

The technical name that Freudenberger and North gave this stage is *revision of values*. In other words, what was once vital to you no longer matters as much. Work has swallowed your life whole.

I know I'm flatlining when Thanksgiving is coming up and instead of making plans to travel and see the kids, I decide to work over the holiday weekend. I know I'm flatlining when I stop wanting to take care of the plants and delegate the job to my husband. I know I'm flatlining when the sight of skis in the closet awakens zero interest in going out on the slopes. I know I'm flatlining when meditation, exercise, being in the kitchen, and going shopping for anything—from food to clothing to gifts—feels boring. I am definitely flatlining, and practically dead, when I lose interest in sex.

How do *you* recognize when you're flatlining?

23

Self-Reflection Exercise #5:
What Did You Once Enjoy Doing?

When I was a kid, we lived about three blocks from a bowling alley. I'd been initiated into the joys of duck-pin bowling by my older brother, Alan (duckpins are the smaller pins found mostly at bowling alleys on the East Coast). Because the balls are also smaller, even children, given enough practice, can get really good at the sport.

I lived to bowl, which is where most of my allowance went.

As I grew older, bowling became less important, but unbeknownst to me, those narrow lanes had left corresponding grooves in my neural circuitry. Many years later, when I'd flatlined once again, Gordie and I happened to drive past a bowling alley. He turned the car around and pulled into the parking lot despite my protestations that I had too much to do and didn't like bowling anyway. However, the simple act of picking up a ball and rolling it down the alley reawakened youthful neural networks primed by possibility, and soon I was laughing and having the time of my life.

You may not remember the joy you once felt in a hobby or activity that has fallen off your radar, so you may need to enlist a friend or loved one in helping you remember. One of my friends who is in her 70s was a dancer in her youth. During a flatline period of her own, she noticed a jazz dance class at her gym and signed up. It was as if a light switch were turned on inside her.

In 1979, Harvard professor of psychology Ellen Langer conducted a fascinating study of how we can improve well-being by doing things we enjoyed in our younger years. She calls it her "counterclockwise study," and you can read more about it in her 2009 book, *Counterclockwise: Mindful Health and the Power of Possibility*. Langer and her colleagues invited two groups of men in their late 70s and early 80s to live in a meticulous re-creation of the year 1959 for one week each. They transformed an old monastery in Peterborough, New Hampshire, into a living time capsule of the world as it was 20 years earlier.

One group was instructed to pretend that the year really was 1959 and talk about "current" events like Castro's victory in Cuba and Nikita Khrushchev and the Cold War in the present tense. The other group spoke of events in the past tense more as observers than participants. All of the volunteers were tested physically and cognitively before the study began and again at its conclusion. While both groups showed increases in strength, flexibility, memory, and intelligence, the group who had acted as if it were really 1959 improved the most. Living like younger versions of themselves actually rejuvenated the men, demonstrating the profound effect that our thinking has on our body.

Think back to a time before you were burned out—when you were at your prime and filled with enthusiasm for life's possibilities. What did you enjoy doing? Choose one activity (like bowling, for example), and put it on your calendar. This is an experiment. If it rejuvenates you, add it to your regular schedule. If it doesn't, choose another activity from an earlier time in your life. Make sure to get out your calendar and actually add this to your schedule.

Stage 6: Frustrated, Aggressive, and Cynical

Humorist and author Loretta LaRoche and I used to give a workshop together that we called "Twisted Sister and The Fairy Godmother." The Fairy Godmother is your idealized self—in the case of women, that usually translates to being sweet, long-suffering, and deeply concerned for the well-being of others. Twisted Sister is her shadow, the "Bitch in the Basement." If you're a guy, you have your own ne'er-do-well equivalent buried in your subconscious. Neither the idealized self nor the shadow is your authentic self—your soul—which is alive, changing, and appropriate to the moment.

The idealized self—the mask you put on for appearance's sake—reaches the breaking point during burnout. All that work to maintain the facade, and it couldn't even deliver the goods. You still don't feel happy and fulfilled. As a result, the false self finally falls off and shatters like a mirror dropped on a tile floor. Then the Bitch (or Bastard) in the basement—the equivalent of the infamous Mr. Hyde—is free to come out and wreak havoc.

This is the point at which you may start yelling at your computer with gusto or devaluing a colleague. The burned-out businessman may focus on the assistant he's always respected and begin to think that he's inept: *Jason takes forever to produce a simple report!* But being disgruntled with Martha is only the tip of the volcano. Underneath a false veneer that is becoming progressively more difficult to hold together, the pressure of frustration is steadily building.

The inner dialogue of a person at this stage is cynical at best, aggressive at worst: *The management around* *here has its head up its ass! That guy who everyone thinks is so great is a #@*&! charlatan. Nice guys finish last around here, so why bother trying to do things right?!*

Regardless of what may be happening around you that's troubling, the biggest problem at this stage of burnout is your own attitude. The good Dr. Jekyll is slowly transforming into the evil Mr. Hyde. You have now succeeded in creating hell not only for yourself but also for the people around you. You've managed to block any real recognition that the situation could be much different if *you* changed.

One of my quarrels with some forms of therapy (I thank my friend and colleague Lee McCormick for this perspective) is that they are aimed at making life in hell a little bit more comfortable. But what is required at this stage of burnout isn't a new pad for the floor of the tent you've pitched in the Inferno; it's packing up and moving on. This requires an authentic curiosity about how you are using your energy.

Self-Reflection Exercise #6: Are You Using Your Energy Efficiently?

A trout catches the majority of its food near the center of a stream. If it swims too far toward either edge, it will use more energy than it takes in and die as a result.

If you're feeling like a tired trout, it's time to take your personal-energy economy more seriously. You'll need to identify what drains you (checking e-mail more than once or twice a day, letting friends or clients suck you dry, signing your kids up for too many activities, spending more money than you need to, and so forth) and what helps you increase the impact of your energy (concentrating on certain aspects of your business, car-pooling with your neighbors, or setting healthy boundaries and enforcing them, for instance).

After you read this section, plan a 30-minute morning writing exercise. Your task is to identify better and more conscious ways to manage your energy. This works best if you're specific, so identify three ways in which you waste energy and three ways to leverage your energy.

Several years before writing *Fried,* I'd signed a contract with another publisher to write a book about slowing down. Unfortunately, I was moving so fast during that period of my life that I couldn't make the time to do it and finally had to return the advance. That's irony for you. Meanwhile, the editor who had recruited me for that project found another person who really knew something about the art of slowing down. His name is Timothy Ferriss, and he wrote a completely dazzling book called *The 4-Hour Workweek,* which is definitely worth reading and putting into action.

Ferriss helped me realize that I was spending too much time on projects that had too little impact. His discussion of Pareto's law, also known in business as the 80/20 Principle, can change your life. The gist is that 80 percent of the effects you get come from 20 percent of the effort you make. For example, 20 percent of your clients may order 80 percent of your widgets; 20 percent of your time spent on social networking might yield 80 percent of your new business; and 20 percent of your time used to exercise, eat well, be with family, and restore yourself may generate 80 percent of the joy in your life.

I checked out the 80/20 rule regarding my public-speaking business. Most of my income does, in fact, come from a minority of my speaking gigs. One-hour keynotes pay well, have the maximum impact in terms of the number of people I reach, and take relatively little time overall. Teleseminars may turn out to be better still, since there's no travel time involved. On the other hand, providing a five-day workshop in a remote retreat center that draws few participants consumes a full week (traveling there and back, as well as preparation) and yields little income. I sometimes choose to do these retreats, but I don't delude myself by calling them business. If they don't return energy to me in the form of enjoyment, I've made a bad bargain.

Every one of us has different leverage points and energy drains. The challenge is to really sit down and identify yours—and then do something about them.

Stage 7: Emotionally Exhausted and Disengaged

As burnout progresses, you possess less and less energy and vitality. The false self has shattered and the resulting emptiness is dispiriting. When your old identity has fallen away and a new one (hopefully, your authentic self) hasn't yet appeared on the scene, you're left without *any* sense of self. Emotionally drained and deadened, exhaustion takes over. There's barely a drop of energy left in you to give to anyone else, and the only respite, paradoxically, is work. Even though you're less efficient and creative than you used to be, your job is something to hang your hat on.

The natural urge at this stage is to isolate and withdraw from friends, family members, and other connections. Individuals who are fried are notorious for feigning illness, taking "mental health days" or actually getting sick. Absenteeism, due largely to health problems, is an enormous drain on the U.S. economy. Mark Pauly, a professor at the University of Pennsylvania's Wharton School, is co-author of a 2006 study that estimated the cost of absenteeism at upwards of $74 billion annually. When you take into account the fact that the great majority of doctor visits are for illnesses or conditions related to stress, it's easy to see why many large corporations are vigilant in the detection and treatment of burnout.

When you reach the stage of withdrawal and isolation where illness becomes a serious issue, drugs—legal or illegal—frequently compound the situation. When you're in emotional or physical pain, it's only natural to want relief. That may come in the form of pain-relieving drugs, sedatives, anxiolytics (anxiety-reducing drugs), narcotics, tobacco, or alcohol. Unfortunately, these solutions often turn into addictions that create significant problems in their own right.

Isolation is a dangerous phase since personal interactions not only function as checks and balances on behavior, but they're also a necessity for maintaining health and emotional well-being. (If you're holed up every night slowly drinking yourself to death, you're more likely to get help if someone knows what's happening.) Social support strengthens immunity, releases feel-good hormones, helps protect cardiovascular health, and keeps the ship of life afloat. Humans are relational animals, which is why the stage of isolation is dire. At this point, reestablishing your social connections is a priority.

Self-Reflection Exercise #7:
Who Do You Tell the Truth To?

Sometimes the person you're most intimate with and can tell the truth to is your spouse, especially if you're a man. One of the reasons why men have an increased incidence of illness and death after they're widowed or divorced is that, in a majority of cases, their wife was their primary confidante. When she's gone, their support system goes with her, and so does their health.

Women, in general, have a wider social support network so that even after the death of a spouse or divorce, statistically speaking, they remain healthier and more emotionally stable. But regardless of gender, the need for intimate communication and honesty is vital for health and well-being. In the latter stages of burnout, the need for social support is of paramount importance. A friend, coach, or therapist is an absolute necessity to keep from completely losing your way. *If you don't have the support you need right now, make a plan to get it.*

Stage 8: "I've Morphed into What?"

You may walk into your living room one day and find a group of family and friends sitting around waiting for your arrival. *Is this a surprise party?* you wonder. Then someone walks out of the kitchen—a stranger with a solemn face bearing neither food nor gifts. You suddenly get it. *This is an intervention.* Not just a friendly sit-down pulled together by a few loved ones, but an organized attempt to get you into a treatment program ASAP because you have now morphed into a bona fide addict.

But substance abuse is not the only substantial change that friends might notice about you. At the height of my last burnout episode, my friend Gayle took me to lunch to tell me that she was seriously worried about me. I was not at all myself. I was withdrawn; emotionally overwhelmed; cynical; fearful; and in her words, in danger of a "total nervous breakdown." At the time, I was running a school to train spiritual mentors, writing a book with my husband, and traveling extensively to teach. Yes, I agreed, I was emotionally exhausted and scattered, but who wouldn't be under those circumstances?

Denial and defensiveness are common throughout the burnout continuum since our entire way of life is on the line. It's nothing short of amazing how fiercely we will defend our pitiful piece of real estate in hell.

But Gayle wouldn't have any of it. She confronted me squarely, pointing out that lately I was either preternaturally calm, like the air before a thunderstorm, or emotionally explosive. "Your life is absolutely not sustainable in this way," she concluded, delivering a clear and powerful friend-to-friend intervention. And that was the truth.

The spiritual-mentor school that I was heading up had me in a dilemma due to a conflict between two of the principals, both of whom I loved. In addition to that, a school is a place where multiple interpersonal conflicts are likely to arise, and I—Queen of the Conflict Averse—am simply not configured to deal with them. Harry Truman once famously quipped, "If you don't like the heat, stay out of the kitchen."

It took another six months for me to realize that I needed to close the school to save myself. And when I did, my energy started to return almost immediately. It was as if I'd been stretched out on a medieval torture rack and someone had finally loosened the screws. What a relief! In no time at all, I recovered and became my old self again. (Well, not quite, since I'm much more careful about avoiding similar situations, as you'll read in the upcoming chapter on burnout-prone temperaments.)

As FBF Gina Vance put it: "We are in relationship with whatever/whomever we are burning ourselves up and out and down with." Ending that relationship, though very difficult, saved my life. The color returned to my cheeks, and I no longer looked or felt like Quasimodo, much to my relief and that of my family and friends.

Self-Reflection Exercise #8: What, Who, and Why?

If whatever is burning me out could be put aside right now, what would that be? Who would I be without that situation? What's stopping me from letting it go? This interrelated triad of *what, who,* and *why* is another 30-minute writing exercise. As you think about these questions, take a few deep breaths and connect with your body. Where do you feel tension, heaviness, or discomfort? As you imagine letting go of the situation, what happens to your body?

Here's a good example of someone who profoundly changed his life after doing the self-reflection exercise and following through. "Jake" was a police officer with multiple physical symptoms: he had gastritis (which causes stomach pain and trouble with digestion) and experienced body aches, insomnia, and intense fatigue. He got anxious every time the dispatcher sent him on a call. Worse still, Jake started to feel like he was losing his edge and becoming a danger to himself and his partner. He was frustrated and angry, and doubtful that things would get any better. There was just too much to do, too few resources, "a lot of lip" (as he put it, from civilians and the media who don't understand what it takes to be a cop), and very few rewards. Furthermore, the work was dangerous and didn't pay particularly well, so Jake also had a second part-time job as a security officer at a bank. He was dining largely on fast food, he missed his family, and he admitted to feeling like he was at the end of his rope.

When Jake did the self-reflection exercise, he realized that letting go of his part-time job would be a huge relief. He could feel the weight sliding off his shoulders just by thinking about it. The *why* he couldn't let go of, however, was the financial aspect. With two kids and a wife to support, he needed the extra income. But when he discussed quitting his second job with his family, they were unexpectedly understanding and supportive. They all agreed that it was far worse to see Jake suffering (and to worry daily about his physical and mental health) than it would be to simplify their lifestyle radically.

Moving to a smaller house, cooking all their meals from scratch, and shopping for clothes at Goodwill would indeed require a major adjustment. But the result was a life far richer in the things that matter most— Jake's improved health and peace of mind, his ability to do his primary job well, and a happier family.

Stage 9: "Get Away from Me!"

People who no longer do their jobs well or simply don't care anymore are suffering from *depersonalization*.

This "screw it" (or sometimes "screw you") attitude is one of the three measurement scales on the Maslach Burnout Inventory (MBI). The MBI, created by Christina Maslach, one of the pioneering researchers of burnout, measures the three major components of burnout: depersonalization, emotional exhaustion, and diminished personal accomplishment.

When you're submerged in the "Get Away from Me!" stage, you start to act with hostility or disinterest toward the very people you're supposed to be helping, seeing them as problems rather than as individuals who need you. You've already lost the connection to your own soul—you're emotionally blunted, miserable, and feeling helpless to change your life. The result is that you can no longer relate to the essential humanity of others.

Depersonalization in the medical field, which we'll use as an example, is called *compassion fatigue*. This is what it looks like: I was a young faculty member in the department of anatomy and cell biology at Tufts Medical School in Boston in the mid-1970s. Justin and Andrei, my two sons, were little guys back then. I'd strained a muscle in the upper-right quadrant of my back lifting them in and out of car and bike seats, backpacks, and cribs. When the strain was still bothering me a few months later, I sought out the faculty health-care services.

I walked into a waiting room so drab and depressing that it could have been located in the Gulag. It was freezing, too. But when I entered the consulting room, I could easily have fainted from the heat. Directly next to the doctor's desk was a space heater that was churning out sufficient BTUs to roast a flock of turkeys. The 30-something doctor was abrupt and dismissive,

radiating waves of emotional exhaustion. I had to resist the ingrained urge of the helper to grab her by the
hand and take her out to lunch where we could talk
as two equals rather than as a burned-out doctor to a
patient. She obviously needed more help than I did.

"What's bothering you?" inquired the depressed doc
while distractedly pulling lint off her sweater (her internal thermostat must have shorted out along with her
compassion). I was clearly an inconvenience that she'd
rather not be bothered with. I explained my symptoms
anyway, ending with the simple question: "How long
do these muscle strains usually take to heal?"

"Let me examine you first," she replied, and I thank-
fully peeled off my sweater. I was nauseated from the
heat. She poked around my spine a little, and I asked
again, "How long until this heals? Do I need physical
therapy or some sort of exercise program? Should I stop
doing yoga for a while?"

"I don't really know," she answered flatly. "It could
be cancer, after all." As a cancer cell biologist and anato-
mist, my knowledge trumped hers hands down. What
an insensitive (not to mention ill-founded) comment
to make to a patient! Fortunately, I knew better, but I
immediately thought of the emotional damage that she
could inflict upon someone who was less well informed.

This young physician obviously didn't give a damn
anymore. Her cynicism and depersonalization were so
advanced that the result bordered on sadism. She did
give me a laugh, though, when she fetched a long ACE
bandage and wrapped it around my torso so that one
breast ended up pointing north while the other pointed south. Her doctoring didn't lead to my relief or to a
great sweater look, so I made my way to the ladies' room

and unwrapped my mummified midriff. The visit was a waste of time for the muscle strain, but it was a sad lesson about what can happen when a heath-care provider burns out.

A 2004 study published in the prestigious *Journal of the American Medical Association* (JAMA) suggests that a significant number of physicians are suffering from burnout. The investigators combed the literature for studies of burnout conducted with the Maslach Burnout Inventory and concluded that the evidence "suggests that the components of burnout may be common among practicing physicians, with 46% to 80% reporting moderate to high levels of emotional exhaustion, 22% to 93% reporting moderate to high levels of depersonalization, and 16% to 79% reporting low to moderate levels of personal achievement."[6]

One of the unfortunate effects of burnout in physicians is dropping out. Just imagine the pain of training for 8 or 12 years at great expense both personally and financially, and then feeling so fried that you give up your profession.

Burnout is an aspect of health-care reform that, in my opinion, needs to be put at the forefront. No matter how well our medical system is funded, if practitioners are fried, their ability to deliver compassionate, excellent care is diminished. Burnout-prevention programs that are instituted in medical or nursing school could make a significant difference to the quality of health care in our country. They need to be based on compassion for oneself—learning what my colleague Cheryl Richardson calls "extreme self-care." Without knowing how to take care of ourselves, the art of caring for others simply cannot flourish.

Self-Reflection Step #9: Compassion Meditation

If you've lost compassion for yourself, it follows that you'll lose it for others as well. Tibetan Buddhists have used specific meditations to cultivate compassion, or *bodhicitta*, for the last 1,700 to 1,800 years. When the stock market crashed in the fall of 2008 and the United States entered what has been called the Great Recession, Dr. Sanjay Gupta, the medical correspondent for CNN, suggested that viewers learn compassion meditation to calm down and counter stress. At that time two new studies (one out of Emory University and the other out of the University of Wisconsin at Madison) demonstrated that compassion meditation could relieve stress; enhance well-being; reduce the inflammatory response, which predisposes us to a variety of illnesses; and even change the happiness set point in the brain.

Compassion meditation begins with sending blessings of loving-kindness to yourself, much as a parent would feel toward his or her beloved child. A basic form of this meditation is: *May I be at peace, may my heart remain open, may I be happy, may I be well.* After you've generated compassion for yourself, send it to your friends, family, co-workers, strangers, enemies, and finally, to all beings.

(You can learn how to practice compassion meditation using my CD *Meditations for Courage and Compassion,* which I released in 2009 as a companion to my book *It's Not the End of the World: Developing Resilience in Times of Change.*)

Stage 10: Inner Emptiness

FBF Laura Flanders wrote this during one of our discussions:

> Coincidentally, a friend posted a quote by Sam Keen right before you on my news feed: "Burnout is nature's way of telling you you've been going through the motions but your soul has departed; you're a zombie, a member of the walking dead, a sleepwalker."

The feeling of having lost yourself is hard to describe, and harder still to live with. The essence of who you are—the way you see the world, your hopes and dreams, your little quirks, the tenderness that you have toward the ones you love—seems to vanish when you're fried. All the attributes of personhood through which you relate to the world disappear as burnout progresses. Who are you when all that goes missing?

The chasm that separates you from life is so vast at this point that stimulation of any kind has to be especially intense to generate any feeling at all. Cruising the Internet for porn, having an affair or unprotected sex, driving drunk, participating in dangerous or extreme sports, engaging in self-mutilation, or signing up for the armed forces on a lark . . . these are all examples of ways to cope with the feelings that you're barely alive and that there's nothing left inside you. At this stage of burnout, you may avoid leisure time because the sense of emptiness is so intense that it's just too painful to be in your own company.

Foods that you once enjoyed may seem flat or uninteresting. A salad, for example, may seem too bland to pique your appetite. But (even if you've been a health-food aficionado) a quart of ice cream, four pieces of fudge, or an entire rack of ribs may temporarily bring you back to life. Powerful, pleasing tastes may bridge the gap between you and sensation far more easily than a plate of steamed vegetables or a poached egg on dry toast.

I ate a lot of bacon (so sorry, arteries) when I was burned out despite the fact that I'd once spent years as a vegetarian and generally eat a healthy diet. Fortunately, you *can* recover your balance by making nutritional choices that will actually help you feel better.

Self-Reflection Exercise #10: What Foods Make You Feel Good?

It's hard to give up behaviors that feel good (even if they're harmful) for ones that feel less rewarding (even if they're beneficial). When my husband and I interviewed the Hindu scholar Swami Adiswarananda for our book *Your Soul's Compass,* he made an important point: None of us renounces what feels good for something that feels worse, but we will happily renounce what we've been doing for something that feels better. The point of this exercise is to find the something that feels better.

Keep track of your food and mood in a very simple way for one week. Stick with your usual diet and, using a scale of 1 to 10 (where 1 is the worst and 10 is the best), rate your overall sense of well-being.

Then at the start of the following week, make *one* healthy change to your diet—whatever is easiest and most sensible for you. It might be eating breakfast if you don't already do so. Maybe it's enjoying a fresh salad for lunch every day. Or how about making sure you're eating five servings of fruit and vegetables daily? At week's end, check out your level of well-being on the 10-point scale.

Was there any difference between the two weeks? If not, try another simple dietary experiment. Sooner or later, you'll be able to renounce what isn't working for something that feels better. A positive side effect of your experiment is that it engages you in the practice of self-care, which is vital to reviving from burnout.

Stage 11: Who Cares and Why Bother?

People who are burned out and hardly give a damn about anything look and feel depressed. But are depression and burnout really the same thing? This is an important question since depressed people are often given powerful drugs with substantial side effects. Do antidepressants work when we're fried? And even if they revive us in the short run, can they help us mend our lives?

Several research teams have asked this question and labored to find some distinction between burnout and depression that's relevant to people's lives rather than just an academic exercise in splitting hairs. Emotional exhaustion is the most salient symptom of both burnout and depression. Fatigue, emptiness, hopelessness, indifference, apathy, and meaninglessness are also obvious overlaps.

Psychologist and burnout expert Veerle Brenninkmeijer and her colleagues at the University of Groningen in the Netherlands do make some distinctions between burnout and depression. They have observed that, compared with depressed individuals, people high in burnout:

(1) make a more vital impression and are more able to enjoy things (although they often lack the energy for it); (2) rarely lose weight, show psychomotoric inhibition (slow down) or report thoughts about suicide; (3) have more realistic feelings of guilt, if they feel guilty; (4) tend to attribute their indecisiveness and inactivity to their fatigue rather than to their illness (as depressed individuals tend to do); (5) often have difficulty falling asleep, whereas in the case of depression one tends to wake up too early.[7]

These distinctions may seem academic, but they make the point that depression and burnout are hard to distinguish and that medicating people for what appears to be depression—rather than helping them with the underlying traits that predispose them to burnout—may be a singular disservice.

Since one in six of us will receive a diagnosis of depression at some point in our lifetime (the reason for this, in large part, is that drug companies have a vested interest in people being diagnosed with depression so that they can be medicated, as we'll discuss in the following chapter), we're losing a lot of very talented human beings to burnout—a preventable and treatable disorder of the soul.

Self-Reflection Exercise #11:
Do You Need Professional Help?

Depression—whether it's related to burnout, grief and loss, overwhelming stress, or biological factors (and these, as you will read, are much rarer than Big Pharma would have you believe)—can be a crippling affliction that needs to be attended to as quickly as possible.

Most people seek help for depression from their family doctor first. Unfortunately, he or she may not be the best source of information and treatment. Most family-practice docs are pressed for time and don't have specialty training in psychiatry. They may, however, be a good source of referral.

If you work for a company that has an EAP (Employee Assistance Program), ask for an appointment because the staff members in these departments are likely to be skilled in the assessment and treatment of burnout. If you don't have access to an EAP, find a mental-health professional in your area who has expertise in both depression and burnout. *You have to be upfront and insistent about getting this information.*

Your helper can be a psychiatrist, psychologist, social worker, nurse-practitioner, or other mental-health professional. Alternative therapies from bodywork to meditation may also be vital for revival, but make sure that you cover all your bases and don't get sidetracked by an alternative or mainstream professional who is a one-trick pony, quickly prescribing antidepressants or supplements or recommending acupuncture, yoga, and so on. While any and all of these may help, none is likely to do the trick on its own.

Finding competent help can seem overwhelming when you're depressed, so you may have to delegate this task, or at least parts of it, to a family member or friend.

Stage 12: Physical and Mental Collapse

Ellen, an international corporate consultant, was so exhausted and strung out that she fainted at the airport while waiting to board a flight to Heathrow. The paramedics—a very efficient crew, so she said—peeled her off the floor and whisked her away in an ambulance. After a trip to the ER revealed nothing more serious than borderline hypertension and exhaustion, she went home and managed to regroup overnight. The next day at 9:05 A.M., she was on a plane to London to meet up with the rest of her team. Like all burnout enthusiasts, Ellen would have felt like a total slacker if she'd taken even one more day to rest and recover.

A few months later, Ellen developed lupus, an autoimmune disease that runs in her family. Nobody can withstand the kind of punishment that she was doling out to herself. While not everyone who succumbs to burnout will develop a serious illness like Ellen did, her outcome is not at all rare. When you tell your body that you're not particularly interested in living, and you let your life force run perilously low, it's not surprising that the physical plant obliges by shutting down.

Like Ellen, some of us will keep on keeping on until our health gives out. And trust me—*it will.* Approximately 70 to 90 percent of visits to family-practice doctors are for problems caused or made worse by stress. And burnout is a source of unrelenting stress and can exacerbate illnesses such as diabetes, cancer, or arthritis. It can also result in allergies, chronic-pain syndromes, immune disorders, digestive problems, anxiety, and depression, among other maladies.

How is it that we can let our life run out like grains of sand from an hourglass and hardly notice that we are nearly gone?

In Dante's *Divine Comedy,* the Inferno is where we come to understand how we got lost in the dark woods of our own life. One of the routes is through *acedia*, a Greek word often associated with the word *sloth* or feelings of apathy and listlessness, but it's really a kind of "spiritual dryness." In the Middle Ages, it often afflicted clerics who were overcome by the sorrow and suffering they encountered. They lost their connection to Spirit and gave up hope. But you don't have to be a member of the clergy to lose touch with the magic and aliveness of the world.

FBF Beverly Potter described the feeling in this way:

> It's a spiritual crisis—a life or death choice. If choosing life, one must somehow dig deep down to find something to grasp and enhance into a revitalizing life force. Certainly those caught up in burnout's vicious cycle (as I call it) hardly remember aliveness. They are dragging. They are depressed, dispirited, unmotivated, despairing . . . they are *down*—shutting down and giving up.

In order to come through such a dry period, we need to find some seeds of renewal—something to grasp and enhance into a revitalizing life force, as Beverly so eloquently put it.

Self-Reflection Exercise #12: Choosing Life

Here is another 30-minute writing exercise to try: write about what means the most to you and how to bring more of it into your life. When I did this, the first thing that came up was spending more time with family—my husband and our children and grandchildren. I travel so much that it's hard to schedule seeing the kids and their families (they all live at a distance), and I'm so tired that the thought of getting on a plane again seems punishing. The answer? We are considering acquiring an RV and driving it around visiting family from March through mid-May, which is "mud season" (the only truly depressing time of year) at home in the mountains of Colorado. The thought of picking up the Phoenix grandkids and driving them to see the California clan revives me. Even doing the research on the various types of RVs is fun and reviving.

The choice to be generative and create a new life or to wither on the vine is yours alone. My hope is that learning more about why particular people burn out and what revives them—which we will continue to discuss in the following chapters—will help you understand your own feelings better and make it easier for you to *choose life* rather than to give in to hopelessness or depression.

Chapter Two

The Depression Industry

"Overheard in a brokerage: 'I worry about economists who are so young that they think the Great Depression was ended by Prozac.'"

— UNKNOWN[1]

I've listened to burned-out colleagues in the health-care profession wrestle with questions like these: *Am I burned out, or do I have a biochemical depression that needs to be treated? Would taking Prozac or an older antidepressant (such as imipramine) help me sleep better and feel more like myself, or would I find it difficult to tolerate like so many of my patients do? I know these drugs are overprescribed, but it can't hurt to give one a try . . . can it?*

In the interest of scientific experimentation—and sincerely hoping to feel better—I asked my family doctor for a Zoloft prescription back in 2001. Within a day I felt distinctly strange, as a kind of buzzing energy seemed to be running through me. Over the next few days, I grew increasingly restless, anxious, and wired— a condition my mother used to describe as "having ants in your pants." Ten days into the experiment, I honestly felt like I was losing my connection with reality. Suspended in between the totally incompatible extremes of mania and zombification, I no longer felt competent to control my own thinking. When a good friend inquired how I was feeling, the best I could come up with was: "*Chemicalized.* I can feel the drug taking over . . . it's like being possessed."

The latter comment is typical of my bizarre sense of humor, by the way, rather than a metaphysical comment suggesting that an exorcism was in order. I was aware of the fact that SSRIs (selective serotonin reuptake inhibitors) can be very hard to tolerate in the first few weeks of treatment, but ten days were enough for this girl. I much preferred to have my old self back again, negative and depressed though she was.

My experience with Zoloft, although not at all unusual, isn't meant to discourage anyone else from trying it under his or her physician's careful supervision. There are thousands (perhaps even hundreds of thousands) of people who credit SSRIs with saving their lives.

In the following pages, we'll explore what antidepressants do and don't do. They may (or may not) be effective for individuals with severe depression, but can they be of help for those who are experiencing the milder spectrum of depression associated with burning out?

In the interest of educating you on what is and isn't known about the science of depression and how it's presented and sold to the public at large, this chapter will take you on a quick tour of the thriving "depression industry."

Let Them Eat Prozac[2]

The primary reason why antidepressants are overprescribed in the U.S. is because depression is overdiagnosed.

When I decided to undertake my experiment with Zoloft, my reasoning went something like this: *I do have a lot of the common symptoms of depression: fatigue, irritability, trouble sleeping, hopelessness, frustration, headaches, body aches, and feeling like a failure. On the other hand, I concentrate well enough and still get pleasure out of skiing, gardening, and being with the kids and grandkids . . . so maybe it's not biological after all. What to do?*

That particular monologue involved ticking off the most commonly published symptoms of depression on my own mental checklist. Just Google "depression symptoms," and self-tests indicating whether you need to seek medical advice will pop up on multiple sites.

The proliferation of online information is due, in large part, to an aggressive campaign on the part of Big Pharma to "educate" doctors and the general public on the epidemic of depression that is supposedly ravishing the nation. It pays to create a market when you have something to sell, even if that something works for unknown reasons and may have serious side effects such as severe anxiety, unmanageable restlessness, sudden weight gain, and obsessive thinking about suicide or homicide (which sometimes leads to terrible tragedy). Yet it can also make a life or death difference to the most severely depressed patients.

Americans use two-thirds of the world's supply of antidepressants. Let's stop to do the math: The U.S. population is currently in the vicinity of 309 million souls, and the world population is about 6.8 billion, which means that approximately 4 percent of the entire planet gobbles up 67 percent of the global supply of antidepressants. That's a veritable river of relief . . . or is it?

The supposed mode of action of the new wave of antidepressants in the SSRI class of drugs is to prevent reuptake of serotonin by synapses in the brain, thus increasing the overall amount of the neurotransmitter available to stimulate neurons. First studied as potential antihypertensive medications, SSRIs (which include Prozac, Zoloft, Celexa, Luvox, Paxil, and Lexapro) were eventually marketed as antidepressants and kicked off a wave of research into a purported link between low serotonin levels in the brain and depression. This is still controversial because low serotonin levels don't seem to affect mood. Furthermore, there's a new antidepressant (tianeptine, which isn't yet available in the United States) that is as effective as the SSRIs, but it actually *lowers* serotonin levels.

Intrigued by what people "on the ground" might have to report about their experiences with SSRIs, I asked that question on Facebook one evening. By the following morning, more than 60 people had weighed in. About a third of the respondents were extremely grateful for the relief that SSRIs (and other types of antidepressants) provided. A few even credited the drugs with saving their lives. Another third reported a partial response to the drugs, several after switching around to different brands over a period of months or years. The final third stated that side effects (the most common being anxiety, restlessness, rapid weight gain, gastrointestinal problems, and rage) were uncomfortable enough that they discontinued the drugs relatively soon after starting them. A few people reported extremely serious side effects, including suicidal thoughts and attempts to end their lives, which were totally new, never having occurred before taking the drugs.

One FBF who is a doctor of Oriental medicine wrote:

> I have had two friends in the last year commit suicide after being put on SSRIs and other antidepressants . . . originally prescribed for pain, not depression. These folks showed no signs of suicidal tendencies beforehand.

These are the kind of cases that finally forced the FDA to implement "black box" warnings about the potentially serious and life-threatening side effects of these drugs.

I'm no stranger to the ways in which drugs affect mood and behavior. While an undergraduate at Bryn Mawr College, I was fortunate enough to take several graduate seminars in psychopharmacology from a Wyeth laboratories research scientist. Their world headquarters was just a short train ride from Bryn Mawr, down the Main Line in Radnor, Pennsylvania. I worked for Wyeth the summer of my junior year and went on to do my honors research there during senior year. Advances in understanding neurotransmitters, brain architecture, and biochemistry; as well as the mechanisms through which drugs affect behavior and mood, were fascinating back in the 1960s, and continue to be so today.

I'm a great believer in the potential of naturally occurring herbal medicines *and* pharmaceuticals to reduce distress when coupled with healing the whole person—understanding the past, dealing with trauma, becoming more mindful/emotionally intelligent, and implementing a healthy lifestyle.

The majority of Facebook comments agreed with that perspective. Even FBFs who felt that antidepressants had

51

been, or still were, lifesaving, stressed the importance of combining them with therapy, exercise, and what one woman called "over-the-top nutrition." Poor eating habits—a hallmark of our fast-paced, fast-food nation—can be clearly linked to fatigue, depression, and diseases that range from diabetes and heart disease to a variety of cancers.

My Facebook wall kept filling up with responses to the SSRI question, as did my private-message mailbox, where about 30 people felt safe enough to recount their personal stories in some detail. One of the common threads that ran through those accounts was a history of childhood incest, physical abuse, sexual abuse, or significant trauma and loss as adults. People who had related this type of story believed that traumatic experiences were at the root of their depression. Some of them reported that the drugs were helpful in calming them down so they could explore these issues. But for others, the drug blunted emotions to such an extent that they blocked access to, and healing from, trauma.

The idea that psychological factors might cause depression was rejected strongly by a handful of FBFs. Why stigmatize people by blaming depression on psychological factors when it's a strictly biological illness, they argued? The metaphor that biological psychiatry commonly invokes—that SSRIs raise serotonin and are needed by depressives in the same way that insulin is needed by diabetics—was cited by two people as proof of the biological nature of the illness.

But it's not so easy to separate the mind from the body. Significant trauma, for example, can cause a lifelong elevation in levels of the stress hormone cortisol that diminishes immune function, scrambles memory, and shrinks the hippocampus (part of the brain's emotional and memory system) and can lead to bad dreams, flashbacks, and depression. These biological problems clearly have a psychological root in post-traumatic stress disorder (PTSD). The argument that SSRIs are a biological treatment for a biological disease is based on the fact that these drugs cause new cells to grow in the hippocampus. So, by the way, do exercise and fish oil, which, like SSRIs, are both as effective as antidepressants for some people but not for everyone.

The bottom line is that depression is a complex condition that is still not completely understood. Some severe types, including bipolar disorder (manic-depressive illness), have a genetic component and are clearly biological. In many cases, they respond well to medication. Earlier I mentioned the clinical psychologist Kay Redfield Jamison, who is a world-renowned expert on manic-depressive illness and has also lived with it personally since her young adulthood. Her best-selling memoir, *An Unquiet Mind*, popularized the disorder and greatly increased public understanding. The problem is that manic-depressive disorder is unlike other forms of depression—apples compared to oranges. Nonetheless, its popularization helped reinforce the idea that all depression is biological and needs to be medicated.

Depression turns out to be a mixed bag, however. Some forms may be biological; but other types are related to grief, burnout, or overwhelming stress. Burnout predisposes individuals to depression, as does trauma. In fact, as we'll explore in the next chapter, it has been documented that adverse childhood experiences increase adult rates of depression by up to 5,000-fold. So how is a busy family doctor, practicing in a community rather than an academic setting, going to sort all of this out? Who should be medicated, when, and with what? And what other kinds of therapy might be effective?

Wow, What a Beautiful Drug Rep!

The vast majority of physicians are neither psychiatrists nor psychopharmacologists who understand the intricacies of biobehavioral research and treatment. Furthermore, the average physician may have too little time to talk with his or her patients and elicit the story of how their symptoms developed and what has been going on in their lives. A patient may complain of stress, trouble sleeping, aches and pains, or a depressed mood, and simply walk out with a prescription for an antidepressant. So great is the fear of "missing" depression and being sued that "defensive medicine" mandates that it's better to be safe than sorry, since depression is now widely thought of as a biological disease requiring medicine to treat it.

How do physicians keep up with all the new drugs that hit the market anyway? A primary source of "continuing education" are manufacturers' representatives (drug reps). These delightful folks appear at the office bearing the modern equivalent of the beads and trinkets with which the Europeans stole Manhattan. They give presentations on new drugs and their usages, and leave the bait in the form of samples. Although it's expensive to deploy this corps of salespeople, it pays off handsomely. Physicians are much more likely to prescribe drugs that have been left as samples. In fact, the return on every dollar spent in this form of direct sales is a little better than ten to one.

The daughter of a good friend of mine was recruited as a drug rep right out of college, as was my youngest son's high-school girlfriend. Both of these young women are beautiful, extroverted, bright, kind, and totally engaging. I can see why they would be hard to kick out of your office. Drug reps are generally attractive young people (college cheerleaders are a group that drug companies often recruit).

Carl Elliott, who teaches at the Center for Bioethics at the University of Minnesota and is the author of several books, including *Better Than Well: American Medicine Meets the American Dream,* wrote an article in *The Atlantic* in 2006 called "The Drug Pushers." He describes drug reps in this way:

> It is probably fair to say that doctors, pharmacists, and medical-school professors are not generally admired for their good looks and fashion sense. Against this backdrop, the average drug rep looks like a supermodel, or maybe an A-list movie star. Drug reps today are often young, well groomed, and strikingly good-looking. Many are women. They are usually affable and sometimes very smart. Many give off a kind of glow, as if they had just emerged from a spa or salon. And they are always, hands down, the best-dressed people in the hospital.[3]

Wow, What Impressive Data!

Appealing young people are undoubtedly driving forces in the world of pharmaceutical sales. Articles ghostwritten by science writers working for drug companies are another. The writers prepare articles drawing on the published research of known investigators and combine it with data that is cherry-picked from other studies, reaching conclusions that are favorable to their company's drugs and which usually discount the possibility of common serious side effects.

When I first read about this practice in the widely lauded book *Let Them Eat Prozac* by David Healy, M.D., I was outraged. (Healy is a psychiatrist, psychopharmacologist, university professor, frequent expert witness, and the former secretary of the British Association for Psychopharmacology.) What happened to medical ethics? How can science writers from companies with vested interests publish "research" that proves the points they want to make yet hides the facts they'd rather forget?

Far from being a critic of psychopharmacology, Healy is one of its most vigorous proponents. He prescribes SSRIs for his own patients when he feels they are a legitimate course of treatment. He has run clinical trials for the manufacturers and has testified for many pharmaceutical companies as an expert witness. He has also been an expert witness for the other side: patients or victims of patients who have been seriously injured by SSRIs.

Currently at the University of Cardiff in Wales, one of Britain's largest teaching and research universities, Healy has run into some predictable problems as a critic of Big Pharma. His views on ghostwriting, the failure of drug companies to report data from unsuccessful clinical trials and overreporting data from successful clinical trials, their habit of covering up potentially lethal side effects, and paying researchers huge sums of money to give lectures that promote their products have earned him the title of the *enfant terrible* of psychiatry.

Healy and others have commented upon the modern movement away from what has been called "psychobabble" (a derisive term for the psychological antecedents of mental-health problems) to "biobabble" (an equally derisive dismissal of biological primacy). The truth clearly lies beyond *babble*—in all of its extremes. Like all of life, human beings are affected by a complexity of interrelated stimuli.

The Movement from "Psychobabble" to "Biobabble"

When I was training to become a clinical psychologist in the late 1970s, some of my scientific colleagues (I was a cancer cell biologist teaching at a medical school when I retrained in psychology) made no bones about suggesting that I'd lost my ever-loving mind.

It's all psychobabble, completely unscientific, some of them insisted, and made the usual Freudian jokes. "No wonder I'm such a data hound," one quipped. "It's all because of my toilet training! I think I'll call my mother right now and say thanks. Or should I be angry at her instead for making me so obsessive that I'm hard to live with?"

These same colleagues changed their tune gradually over the years. They became fascinated with advances in neurobiology and the emergent understanding that brain circuitry isn't set in stone—it can be changed by experience and behavior. My stock definitely went up, since scientists like science.

Psychiatry has long been considered unscientific—the impoverished stepchild of the other medical specialties. Modern medicine is based on understanding the etiology (the causation or origin) of illness and offering treatments to correct the underlying causes. The cardiologist can trace high blood pressure to various, mostly treatable, roots. The endocrinologist can prescribe weight loss, nutritional change, and exercise to reverse type 2 diabetes, or insulin to manage type 1 diabetes. The gastroenterologist can diagnose an ulcer and prescribe an antibiotic to knock out the bacteria that caused it. But psychiatry hasn't had a biological basis until recently.

Freud and Jung, while fascinating and insightful, couldn't reliably put their finger on a biological cause for anxiety, depression, or psychosis and then prescribe a cure based on evidence acquired from research. Both engaged in what some people derided as psychobabble. And interestingly, some of those individuals are now promoting *biobabble,* citing research that is inconclusive in order to appear "evidence based," which is the currency of modern medicine.

The Hippocratic oath, which all physicians take, includes the vow never to do harm. But in the case of drug treatment for depression, most physicians are still unaware of the harm that they may inadvertently cause. Under the sway of biobabble and the convincing tactics of drug companies, they may be unaware of the specific risks and benefits of antidepressants. Therefore, understanding them as a consumer, even if your physician doesn't, is critically important as you do everything you can to revive from burnout.

Please note: I am not making a case either for or against taking antidepressant medication. That is a decision that only you can make in collaboration with a physician who knows you well and understands your health history, symptoms, and life circumstances. All

I urge is that you take the time to find the right physician to work with in managing your depression.

The Unexplained Risks of SSRIs

I hesitated to include this section at first because it's controversial and disturbing. But for the sake of completeness, I believe it's vital to address the entire antidepressant conundrum. Dr. Healy, who was an early adopter of SSRIs, soon noticed alarming side effects in some of his patients, including intense agitation, restlessness, high anxiety, obsessive thinking, and suicidal/homicidal thoughts and tendencies. There is no longer any question that Prozac and other SSRIs can sometimes cause a small minority of patients at low or no risk of suicide to kill themselves or become homicidal and kill others, often within days of beginning treatment.

While the majority of people on SSRIs will *not* commit suicide or turn into murderers, even my small, unscientific Facebook sample of about 60 people revealed the following: one person had to quit Prozac because it enraged her; two suicides were reported by a third party in people taking antidepressants for pain who weren't even depressed; one woman attempted suicide; one woman reported that her husband became significantly more suicidal than he'd been before treatment on a cocktail of antidepressants; and one woman stated that Prozac put her in what she called a "dangerous state of mind," saying that "I could see how some people can commit suicide or homicide while on it."

The SSRI Withdrawal Support Site, which is based in the U.K., is dedicated to compiling incidents of homicides and suicides that may be linked to SSRIs.

The site includes dozens of cases such as:

> Christopher Pittman, aged 12 (Paxil then Zoloft). Known amongst family as "Pop-Pop's shadow", he had always been very close to his grandfather. Shortly after being prescribed Zoloft he shot both his grandparents dead and burned the house down. Imprisoned, he waited 3 years for trial, and was then tried as an adult—a practice acceptable in the USA.[4]

Such sites are controversial, as is the possible effect of SSRIs on homicides. I Googled Christopher Pittman and discovered a Website created by his supporters, which displays a running clock tracking the days, hours, minutes, and seconds that he has been incarcerated. At the time of this writing, he was 19 years old and still in jail (he'd been given a 30-year sentence). According to the site, before being sent to live with his grandparents, he endured an unstable, chaotic home life and was prescribed Paxil and then Zoloft (apparently at higher-than-normal dosages) after threatening to kill himself. He has recently been granted another trial, and the jury is out as to whether or not the SSRIs provoked his homicidal actions.

Other people have fared somewhat better than this very unfortunate young man, at least in the eyes of the law. The U.K. Website lists several cases that concern seemingly mild-mannered individuals who underwent radical personality transformations, such as the following:

> Donald Schell [aged 60] (Paxil). 48 hours after starting Paxil, he killed his wife, daughter, grand-daughter and himself. *(Jury found Paxil at cause and ordered*

GlaxoSmithKline to pay $6.4 million to surviving family members.)

David John Hawkins, aged 76, Australia (Zoloft). Strangled his much-loved wife with no warning. *(Judge found: "I am satisfied that but for the Zoloft he had taken, he would not have strangled his wife".)*[5]

Among the most famous homicidal activity that may or may not be connected with SSRIs involves Eric Harris, one of the teenagers responsible for the Columbine High School murder/suicide tragedy in 1999. Journalist Christopher Bollyn told the story of Mark Taylor, one of the first students shot. Taylor tried to sue Solvay, the international pharmaceutical company that produces Luvox (an SSRI) but was eventually dissuaded by threats of a libel countersuit, according to Bollyn, who also wrote the following:

In early 1998, according to [Mark] Taylor's lawsuit, [Eric] Harris had taken Zoloft for two months, but soon became "obsessional." Harris became obsessed with homicidal and suicidal thoughts "within weeks" after he began taking Zoloft. . . . Due to his obsession with killing, Harris was switched to Luvox [the same class of drug], which was in his system at the time of the shooting, according to his autopsy.[6]

Suicide, Depression, and SSRIs

To reiterate what I said earlier, most people who use SSRIs don't commit suicide or turn into murderers, and many are helped. But there is still much to be learned about the marketing of drugs and how that market is created and sustained. Since the first reports of suicides linked to SSRIs were made public, drug companies have consistently discounted them in court and in written publications, arguing that those taking them were depressed to begin with and therefore already at a high risk for suicide.

According to Healy, they used data—which is still seen today on many mental-health Websites—stating that the lifetime risk of suicide for a depressive is 15 percent. In fact, I cited that same data in my last book (*It's Not the End of the World: Developing Resilience in Times of Change*). The fear of missing a case of depression or not treating it adequately and having a patient commit suicide is daunting. That 15 percent statistic is compelling for health-care providers *and* patients. Who would want to forego medication with those odds? And what physician would want to risk a malpractice suit—or much worse, a patient's suicide—by failing to provide what is widely believed to be "evidence-based" antidepressant drug therapy?

The classic article that generated the scary 15 percent suicide figure was a two-page meta-analysis (a study of studies) of severely depressed hospitalized patients published in *The British Journal of Psychiatry* in 1970 by Samuel Guze and Eli Robins, working out of Washington University in St. Louis. More recent studies have revised that figure downward substantially. According to a report on suicide prevention by the U.S. Department of Health and Human Services: "Best estimates are that suicide rates among those who had previously been treated for a depressive disorder as inpatients are about twice as high (4.1%) as those who had been treated as outpatients (2%)."[7]

As Healy notes, *hospitalized patients with severe depression are not the ones given Prozac in clinical trials.* Those patients experienced mild and moderate depression that physicians in family practices are likely to encounter and treat—the kind you may experience in burnout. In an attempt to estimate the rate of suicide in depressed individuals in the community whose illness was too mild to warrant hospitalization, Healy and his colleague Jed Boardman arrived at an estimate of less than 30 suicides per 100,000 patient years for depressives in primary care. That means, for example, that if 10,000 patients were followed for 10 years (equaling 100,000 patients years) there would be 30 suicides in that group.

In contrast, a study of patients on Prozac cited by Healy documented 272 suicides per 100,000 patient years for people in their first month on Prozac. This translates to a ten-times greater relative risk of suicide for people with mild depression being treated with Prozac, which is marketed through the ironic scare tactic that without it . . . depressed patients are much more likely to commit suicide!

Antidepressants vs. Placebos

One of my pharmacology professors at Harvard Medical School in the late 1960s counseled our class to stick with prescribing older drugs whenever possible. A lot of patients respond to new drugs, he opined, due to the "placebo effect," which is when patients respond to placebos (a "fake" treatment, such as a sugar pill or saline solution) because they believe that their medication will be effective. In other words, they think it will work, so it does. (In studies of individuals given mild electric shocks, for instance, those who believed that they were given a numbing cream beforehand reported that they felt less pain. The pain centers in their brain, highlighted with brain-imaging technology, actually showed less activity. *Belief becomes biology.*) Furthermore, my professor maintained, the long-term side effects of new drugs are unknown, so it's best to stick with the tried-and-true.

The economic difficulty with my professor's practical and reasonable approach, of course, is that drug companies don't make any money from pharmaceuticals that have outlasted their patents and flood the market as cheap generics. And more and more, economic considerations rule, or at least play a major part, in the big business of medicine. After all, antidepressants were a $9.6 billion business in 2008.

It's also important to note that some people who pursue lifestyle changes, therapy, and other measures simply aren't helped. They *only* respond to antidepressants.

This wide variation in response is why the treatment of depression is far from an exact science. It's an experiment that proceeds through trial and error. What works for one person may not work for another. And what *once* worked for a person may quit working altogether in a matter of months or a year or two.

A question that several SSRI researchers have asked is the degree to which a patient's belief in the efficacy of a drug might influence the results of treatment. When patients trust that a medication will work, 30 to 60 percent get better even if they're given a sugar pill. This is the placebo effect in action, and it's a cornerstone of mind-body medicine.

Research scientists, including Healy, have wondered how much of the improvement in symptoms ascribed to SSRIs might occur due to the placebo effect. Healy points out that these drugs are powerful, changing brain chemistry and behavior. I can attest to that. My response to Zoloft was distinctly chemical. But are they really antidepressants, and if so, in which populations do they work—those with mild, moderate, severe, or very severe depression?

In February 2008, the psychologist Irving Kirsch, working at the University of Hull in the U.K., published a study that involved collaborators at several universities in the U.S. and abroad. Together, they fired a shot that was *not* heard round the world—and may never be. They found that SSRIs were no better than placebos except in the most severe cases of depression. In their abstract, the investigators summarized the impact of unpublished studies that drug companies were required to report to the FDA by law, but had never released to the academic community or general public. (Now you can understand why Healy insisted that not including such studies is bad science that masks poor results.) This is the conclusion that Kirsch and his co-authors made:

> Meta-analyses of antidepressant medications have reported only modest benefits over placebo treatment, and when unpublished trial data are included, the benefit falls below accepted criteria for clinical significance. . . .
>
> [Our] findings suggest that, compared with placebo, the new-generation antidepressants do not produce clinically significant improvements in depression in patients who initially have moderate

or even very severe depression, but show significant effects only in the most severely depressed patients.[8]

This study wasn't Kirsch's first salvo. Back in 1998, he and colleague Guy Sapirstein of the University of Connecticut analyzed data from 38 manufacturer-sponsored studies, which showed significant improvement in 3,000-plus patients taking SSRIs and other types of antidepressants. Patients on placebos, however, showed almost the same level of response. Even after their findings were published, though, the romance with antidepressants continued. Over the next decade, the number of people taking them actually doubled.

Shortly after I finished drafting this chapter, the cover of the February 8, 2010, *Newsweek* announced "The Depressing News About Antidepressants." *Newsweek*'s crackerjack science editor Sharon Begley began her article with these words: "Studies suggest that the popular drugs are no more effective than a placebo. **In fact, they may be worse.**" (The bolding is *Newsweek*'s, not mine.)

Begley's article begins with a moral conundrum that has been bothering me since I first decided to include this chapter in the book. Can reports that antidepressants are no more effective than a placebo (at least for all but the most severely depressed patients) do harm?

If your depression is responding well to medication and then you find out that the result is due to your *belief* in the efficacy of the drug rather than the drug itself, will your depression return? No one knows the answer to that, but my bet is that those helped by the drugs won't be bothered by the data on the placebo response.

When I discussed this subject with a medically astute friend, her jaw dropped. Her husband had been taking Prozac for 15 years and credits it with giving him his life back. I didn't ask, but I suspect that she won't be sharing Kirsch's study or this chapter with him. Why upset the applecart? But even if my friend did, it might not matter. In one study cited by Kirsch, patients who found out that they were responding to a "dummy pill" for pain demanded to keep on taking it. After all, it worked just fine.

A couple of months after Kirsch's new book, *The Emperor's New Drugs,* which delves deep into the effectiveness of antidepressants, was released in 2010, I spoke to another knowledgeable colleague about it. He had heard nothing at all about either the book or the studies. This, of course, is the problem with modern research. There's a lot of it. And unless you're a research scientist, or have a particular interest in a topic, relevant studies may not cross your desk for a very long time. Even if they do, you might not have the expertise to vet them or the nerve to act on them.

Sharon Begley ends her article with an intriguing question: *Is it more important to know the truth or let sleeping dogs lie?* Kirsch thinks that if people know the truth about antidepressants, it might motivate them to try other forms of treatment first. Begley isn't so sure. Based on the reception that Kirsch's work got over a decade ago, it may be that people (including physicians) simply don't pay attention to what they don't want to know, or what contradicts their observations.

The question that holds the most interest for me, however, is *why* a placebo can relieve depression. It's clearly not a direct biological effect, but an indirect one—no less powerful—that is the result of hope. Since depression is, by definition, a disorder of hope (a giving up and letting go of life), it's remarkable that we can return to life so quickly, only because we believe it's possible.

Cognitive-behavior therapy (CBT), overall, has a better track record than drugs in treating depression and preventing its recurrence. This practice is aimed at changing patients' minds and getting them to question the reality of their negative beliefs: *Is it really true that your life is worthless and that you've run out of options?*

University of Pennsylvania psychologist Martin E.P. Seligman, the founder of modern positive psychology, has contended that disputing your pessimistic thought pattern can help lift depression. The National Association of Cognitive-Behavioral Therapists defines the craft in this way:

> Cognitive-behavioral therapy is based on the idea that our *thoughts* cause our feelings and behaviors, not external things, like people, situations, and events. The benefit of this fact is that we can change the way we think to feel/act better even if the situation does not change.[9]

Drugs, perhaps, should be reserved for those for whom other treatments such as CBT are ineffective. The problem is, of course, that most people would prefer to pop a pill rather than engage in self-reflection and make lifestyle changes.

Please let me remind you again that *if you are depressed and taking an SSRI or other antidepressant, under no circumstances should you discontinue it without consulting with your physician.* You may be someone who benefits from the drug. In addition, withdrawal can be severe. Although SSRIs were developed as a response to the addictive potential of benzodiazepines

(Valium, for example), they've turned out to be even more addictive. These drugs must be tapered off very slowly—and only under expert medical supervision—to avoid potential side effects such as extreme emotional lability, nightmares, severe anxiety, depression, hallucinations, short-term memory loss, suicidal/homicidal thinking, or blackouts.

Exercise as an Antidepressant

If SSRIs don't always work, what alternatives are there to treating depression? The best are cognitive-behavioral therapy (as previously discussed); regular exercise; and a newer treatment called "hope therapy," which helps people set goals and take reasonable steps toward accomplishing them.

My favorite alternative treatment is exercise. Studies of individuals with mild to moderate depression—many of whom were doubtless suffering from burnout in the first place—have demonstrated that regular physical activity is superior to SSRIs in ameliorating depression. My personal experience is that if I don't exercise, I'm much more likely to suffer from moodiness and low-level depression.

In a study comparing Zoloft to working out, volunteer patients who were between the ages of 50 and 77 were divided into three groups. The first group exercised only: they rode a stationary bike, walked, or jogged for 30 minutes three times a week. The second group received the drug alone and didn't exercise, and the third group exercised and took Zoloft. At the end of 16 weeks, all three groups showed significant and equivalent improvement, suggesting that consistent physical activity can relieve depression all by itself. And its side effects include better health and a longer life.

It's vital to keep in mind, however, that what alleviates depression in one person may not help you. You need to find out what works best for you, as "Phyllis" did, who is a dear friend of mine and an accomplished artist and philanthropist. Anxious and depressed for most of her life (as was her physician father before her), Phyllis self-medicated with alcohol for many years until addiction finally brought her to AA. Neither antidepressants nor psychotherapy, unfortunately, were of any use in treating her depression, and she could never mobilize herself to exercise regularly. At the end of the day, only my friend's strong spiritual belief in a Higher Power and working the 12 steps have kept her going.

There are many people like Phyllis for whom unexplained biological factors seem to be the primary cause of depression. But childhood experiences, stress, diet, and different levels of social support can affect the expression of genetic potential for better or worse. Some of the major predictors of both burnout and depression, it turns out, are adverse childhood experiences.

Let's turn our attention to these, and take a closer look at the ways in which they predispose us to feelings of helplessness and wanting to give up.

Chapter Three

The Childhood Roots of Burnout

"There can be no keener revelation of a society's soul than the way in which it treats its children."

— NELSON MANDELA

Burnout and depression don't spring forth whole like Athena from the head of Zeus. They grow in emotional soil polluted by helplessness that was deeply rooted in the nervous system during childhood. Given the right conditions—a bad economy, a mismatch of values at work, frequent rejection, an abusive or loveless relationship, or a world gone berserk—those seeds of burnout and depression often germinate many years later. While the immediate problem seems to stem from current circumstances, the ground that nourished it was tilled long ago.

As you read this chapter, reflect upon your own childhood experiences. If they're at the root of your burnout and depression, healing them is a high priority. Taking pills may reduce your distress, but trauma that was hardwired into your nervous system as a child needs to be identified and rewired. While anyone can go through periods of stress and helplessness that culminate in burnout, some people (including me) who endured intense

71

childhood episodes of helplessness are much more prone to periods of burnout as adults.

How I Learned to Be Helpless

I was seven years old when my blissful childhood innocence was lost . . . or more properly, was torn away. My protective Jewish mother had rigorously researched overnight summer camps, and I was duly dispatched to the famous (or so my mother said) "Camp Sunrise Lake," where my bunk mates, who were a year older, derived enormous pleasure from my systematic torment. These little girls were bullies of the first order in a time before the long-term negative effects of bullying were understood.

Kids who are bullied tend to have low self-esteem and develop "learned helplessness," the feeling that changing one's situation is improbable or even impossible. That internalized sense of helplessness, in turn, leads to feelings of hopelessness, apathy, and depression in adulthood. The operative mind-set is that life is a trap, and you are the prey.

My pint-size tormentors tossed my tennis balls into the woods, humiliated me in sexually explicit games of doctor, and excluded me from their conversations. I complained to Carol—a particularly wimpy and ineffectual counselor—who, unbelievably, did nothing at all. Next I complained to the camp director, whose niece happened to be the torturer-in-chief, and she didn't do anything either. I wrote home, but my letters were confiscated "for my own good." I got the message that *I* was a bad person, and it was best that my parents be protected from that distressing knowledge.

Still indignant rather than helpless, I took matters into my own hands. One moonlit night I donned a dress for camouflage and stuffed all my gear into a long green duffel bag. I ducked under the searchlight beams, which rhythmically scanned the periphery of the property, and made a run for it. I walked all night in the general direction of where I thought home might be, dragging the heavy duffel bag behind me. At the time, I didn't realize that its contents weren't limited to my clothes and tennis racket. Also in that bag was my sense of agency in the world—that "I can do it" feeling. And it was as heavy as lead and would take me years to unpack.

By the morning, I knew I had to call my parents and tell them what was happening so they could pick me up. Still filled with the innocent trust of a seven-year-old, I knocked on the door of a homey cottage seeking help. I needed a glass of water and access to a telephone. The lady of the house seemed gentle and kind in her floral housedress with her hair pinned up in spit curls. Her brow crinkled as she listened to my story, and she shook her head in troubled disbelief. Then she disappeared into the kitchen, ostensibly to make breakfast before we called my parents. I sat in a chair by the window, safe in the thought that my parents would soon be there.

In a matter of minutes, the sound of tires crunching on gravel trumpeted a destiny that neither my parents nor I had foreseen when I'd been sent off to a camp for privileged young ladies. The dusty white station wagon marked Camp Sunrise Lake pulled into the driveway. I'd been caught, betrayed by the harmless-looking Housedress Lady.

It took just a few minutes to drive back. The car rolled slowly through the rear entrance past garbage bins and a pile of old construction materials poking out from under a tarp. The place was quiet, since almost everyone was in the mess hall eating breakfast. I was marched in, and there was sudden silence as 150 or so pairs of eyes looked up and tracked my progress.

"Stand up on that table, and don't move a muscle until lunch," is about the only dialogue I remember. Too shocked to cry and much too young to understand that I was the victim of a cruel camp director (who herself must have been victimized by malicious caretakers), I stood on the empty table for hours.

Thus began a month of punishment in semi-solitary confinement. I was held prisoner in my bunk unless it was mealtime. No swimming, no games, no rehearsals for the big play. I did become a champion jacks player, excelling in the fine art of solitary amusement. My letters home continued to be censored, and I was informed that if I ever told anyone about what had happened, my parents would instantly know what a terrible person I was and would surely reject me. I would be homeless and abandoned, revealed as the ugly creature that I'd been all along without knowing it.

My small world hung on a slender vow of silence, which lasted for several months until dinner one dark winter's evening at our apartment in Brookline, an urban suburb of Boston. With a big smile that made the corners of his blue eyes crinkle, my father proudly announced that the family finances were in good-enough shape to send me back to Camp Sunrise Lake for another summer of wholesome fun and frolic.

First I held my breath and shut my eyes. Then in a rush of hot tears, the whole story spilled out of me. My parents sat still and listened from start to finish. Remarkably, they didn't hate me after all, nor did they accuse me of exaggerating or making the story up. My mother even refrained from calling me Sarah Heartburn, which she always did if I was emotional about anything.

When I'd finally heaved a last jagged sigh of relief, my mother rose from her chair like an avenging angel. She was a formidable force—outspoken, fearless, and as relentless as a bloodhound. With her huge blue eyes narrowed and nostrils flared, she calmly assured me that the camp director's wagon would be fixed good first thing in the morning. I would have loved to have heard *that* conversation.

The Long-Term Effects of Helplessness

Although the loving and protective response of my parents was a tremendous relief, it wasn't enough to neutralize the feelings of helplessness and hopelessness that I'd lived with for several weeks, before and after solitary confinement. Before camp (BC) I'd been a spunky little kid; after camp (AC), I grew withdrawn and tentative, afraid of rocking the boat or calling attention to myself.

"Why can't you be more like your friend Judy?" my mother asked one day when I was about ten. "She's a natural." I felt embarrassed and angry. Once upon a time—BC—I *was* a natural. But AC, I never made a move without mentally rehearsing it first. The world felt dangerous, and it was hard to know just how to act to avoid some awful fate. I became shy and insecure at the very time in the cycle of development when young girls should be at the pinnacle of their power.

The seeds of what psychologist Martin Seligman refers to as learned helplessness had been sown. Well before the time of adolescence—when vibrant young girls suddenly go quiet and temporarily fade into the woodwork—some essential part of me had already disappeared.

What exactly is learned helplessness? Consider this experiment: Three rats are put in a small chamber with a lever. Rat #1 can learn to press the lever to turn off mild electric shocks delivered to a metal grid on the bottom of the cage. Rat #2 is called a "yoked control." When the first rat presses the lever, the shock turns off for the second rodent as well. Both animals get exactly the same amount of discomfort. The essential difference, however, is that the second rat isn't in control of its environment. The shock goes on and off on its own whether Rat #2 turns in circles or whistles the rodent equivalent of Dixie. Rat #3 isn't shocked at all and serves as a control for the stress of being handled and confined to a small space. In just a few days, one of the rats will develop bleeding ulcers. Which one do you think it is?

If you said Rat #2, you're right. Having control rescues the first rat from stress; in fact, it makes Rat #1 even more resilient biologically. Rising to a challenge—as long as you can overcome it—is a positive experience. Rat #3, having never endured being shocked, isn't all that stressed. But Rat #2 is made helpless, and animals that are helpless become hopeless. They lose the will to act. If the helpless rat is then put into the first chamber, it actually takes Rat #2 much longer than a naïve rat (one who has never been in this experimental situation) to learn how to turn off the electric shock. Rat #2 has learned to be helpless and may never master the art of controlling its environment.

Helpless rats are also prone to a variety of physical ills. They are, for example, less able to reject implanted tumors, in part because of deficits in immune function. They may also die suddenly from a heart attack. People who have learned to be helpless often suffer similar fates. Viktor Frankl wrote about helplessness, the loss of immune function, and sudden cardiac death suffered by inmates in the Nazi death camps of World War II.

Renowned psychiatrist George Engel developed a "biopsychosocial" model of health and illness in the 1950s, documenting the role of helplessness and hopelessness as precursors to physical illness and early death. More recent research is documenting the biological pathways through which this happens.

Learned helplessness can be induced in situations far less dire than concentration camps. For example, college students who volunteered for a psychological study were put at desks and warned that a loud noise would soon come on. Half of the students had a panic button to push if the noise got too loud, and the other half didn't. The group that had buttons never used them, since the perception of control was sufficient enough to make the noise tolerable. All of the students were then asked to fill out a questionnaire about their experience in a room with very bright lights. Those who didn't have panic buttons in the first part of the experiment were more anxious and less likely to turn down the lights in the room than the students who believed that they could have turned off the noise at any time.

But here's an interesting twist: Not all the students lacking panic buttons became helpless. Their response was dependent upon their thinking style, which was in place long before the experiment. Those who were easily made helpless, according to Dr. Seligman, had a pessimistic mind-set, which he believes is the cognitive root of depression. The more optimistic thinkers, in contrast, experienced more control over their environment.

Contrary to popular usage, pessimism is more than a negative view of the future; it's an explanatory style that is deeply rooted in a person's neurological makeup. Specifically, if something bad happens, how do you explain it to yourself? A pessimist has an explanatory style that features the three *P*'s: *personal, pervasive,* and *permanent* thinking.

Let's say that Pessimistic Peter's girlfriend breaks up with him. He's likely to take it *personally* and blame himself. "I always do the wrong thing," he says. "I'm clueless when it comes to girls."

Furthermore, Peter's self-talk centers on being a loser not just with girls, but generally speaking. He could get better grades, be better looking and more popular, and have more money. That's *pervasive* thinking. Instead of focusing on the problem at hand—the breakup—in Peter's world, *everything* is wrong.

Bad things *always* happen to poor, miserable Peter. His life is a *permanent* disaster area. Seligman sums up Pessimistic Peter's style as: "It's my own fault, I mess up everything I do, and it's the story of my life."

Something happened during the formative years of individuals such as Peter to disempower them. They lost *agency*—the ability to change the world around them. Helplessness may come in the form of a sadistic camp director; a parent who is unpredictable (or one who leaves or dies); or a sexual, emotional, or physical abuser who functions like an inescapable electric shock.

Your brain develops neural pathways as you mature. If learned helplessness is part of that maturation, it becomes a robust biological predictor of behavior, thinking style, health, and burnout.

Mind-Body Medicine

When I was in hospital practice as a psychologist and medical researcher, many of my colleagues looked on those of us interested in psychological factors and disease as "soft scientists" at best. As I've mentioned, psychologists (and psychiatrists, too) were on the low end of the academic totem pole. According to the critics, we didn't do "real" medicine; we just poked around in people's childhoods and blamed their mothers.

Old-style psychosomatic medicine, which posited familial problems as a risk factor for everything from juvenile insulin-dependent diabetes to asthma, gradually gave way to the more modern specialty of behavioral medicine in the 1970s. The field of psychoneuroimmunology, for example, describes links among emotional states, hormones, brain function, immune factors, and illnesses. A brief look at the type of research being done in the field will set the stage for a better understanding of how stress and learned helplessness contribute to various diseases and premature death—including the health problems created by burnout.

Psychologist Janice Kiecolt-Glaser, a colleague of mine since the mid-1980s, is a professor of psychiatry and psychology at Ohio State University; and has authored more than 175 articles, chapters, and books, often collaborating with her husband, Dr. Ronald Glaser (who is the director of the Institute for Behavioral Medicine Research). Kiecolt-Glaser's research is evidence based and shows that stress accelerates age-related changes in interleukin-6 (IL-6), an immune factor called a cytokine. High levels of IL-6 are linked to cardiovascular disease, type 2 diabetes, osteoporosis, arthritis, frailty, the functional decline of aging, and some cancers.

The older you are, says Dr. Kiecolt-Glaser, the more that stress matters. It even weakens your response to immunizations. And if you're married but not getting along with your spouse, beware. It will take longer for your wounds to heal than it would if you weren't so stressed out. And if you're a caretaker for someone with Alzheimer's disease (this heartbreaking situation is often used as a naturally occurring model of stress), your IL-6 levels may be up to four times higher than average. What you experience emotionally directly affects your health.

The Effects of Adverse Childhood Experiences

Enter Dr. Vincent J. Felitti, the director and founder of the Department of Preventive Medicine at the Kaiser Permanente Medical Group in San Diego. He and his colleague Robert Anda, M.D. (from the Centers for Disease Control and Prevention in Atlanta) have hammered the last nail in an argument that's been bandied around for years: whether or not adverse events in childhood predict health in later life. The ACE (Adverse Childhood Experiences) study is a major research project that investigates the ways in which childhood experiences have affected health decades later.

The ACE study began with a curious observation. In the mid-1980s the Kaiser Permanente Department of Preventive Medicine noticed that one of their obesity programs had a high dropout rate. Oddly, many of those who left the study had actually lost weight. To the surprise of the investigators, who conducted in-depth life interviews with 286 of those individuals, childhood abuse turned out to be a very common theme in the patient narratives. When individuals reported being abused, they were likely to comment that their weight gain had started shortly thereafter. A number of patients said that they'd made an association between their abuse and the obesity years before, but when they had pointed it out to their doctors, they were discounted. The abuse was so long ago, after all. How could it still be affecting them 10, 20, 30, 40, or even 50 years later?

The obesity, according to Dr. Felitti, wasn't their problem. It was, in fact, their *solution*. He cites the case of a woman who was raped and gained over a hundred pounds that year: "Overweight is overlooked, and that's the way I want to be," she said.[1]

Felitti's response to the stories of his patients is both insightful and compassionate:

> We saw that things like intractable smoking, things like promiscuity, use of street drugs, heavy alcohol consumption, etc., these were fairly common in the backgrounds of many of the patients. . . . These were merely techniques they were using; these were merely coping mechanisms that had gone into place.[2]

The Department of Preventive Medicine where Dr. Felitti made his observations kept detailed records of psychological, social, and biomedical data for more than 55,000 members, most of whom were middle-class Americans. It's a sad fact that 22 percent of this population reported childhood sexual abuse on their questionnaires. When asked subsequently, "How did that affect you later in life?" their responses, Felitti found, often provided important clues about how best to approach the treatment of their adult ills.

Felitti and Anda asked 26,000 consecutive adult patients if they would be interested in helping them understand how childhood events might have affected their health, and 68 percent agreed to be included in the study.

This large group of willing patients helped the researchers identify eight categories of adverse experience: the three abuse categories were emotional, physical, or sexual; and the five categories of household dysfunction included living in a home where there was violent treatment of the mother, a substance abuser, a household member in prison, a chronically depressed or mentally ill household member, or the loss of a biological parent through any cause. If a person wasn't exposed to any of these eight categories of ACE, they scored a zero. Otherwise, one point was given for each kind of adverse experience.

Since the average age of participants was 57, the researchers were looking at the association between current health and childhood experiences that occurred as far back as a half century prior. What they discovered was that *time doesn't heal. It only conceals the roots of illness and dysfunction due to adverse childhood experiences.*

If all physicians were trained to identify and understand the effects of early childhood experiences on health and well-being, the savings both in human suffering and health-care dollars would be astronomical. As Dr. Anda commented:

> I think of my training as a medical student; I learned nothing of this. I think every medical student should

be taught about adverse childhood experiences, abuse, violence, and neurodevelopment, and how the consequences will lay hidden right in front of their eyes unless it's a standard part of medical care to inquire about it.[3]

Just over 50 percent of the Kaiser Permanente patients had ACE scores of 1 or above. One in four had scores of 2 or higher; one in 16 had scores greater than 4. Total ACE scores predicted future mental and physical health, as well as behaviors such as drug abuse, smoking, and alcohol abuse in a most remarkable way—there was a direct correlation. The higher the ACE score, the more serious the adult health and behavioral problems.

Take cigarette smoking—and for many years, I wish someone would have taken mine! I must have quit a thousand times (sometimes succeeding for a few years and then relapsing again) before I finally quit for good. My own ACE score, by the way, is at least a 3 and perhaps a 4. My father was depressed, my mother was a genteel alcoholic, a service person sexually abused me, and then there was the emotional abuse at Camp Sunrise Lake.

A person with an ACE score of 4 is 390 percent more likely to develop chronic obstructive pulmonary disease (COPD), which is strongly related to smoking. There is a similar relationship between a high ACE score and hepatitis. Patients with an ACE score of 4 have a 240 percent higher chance of developing hepatitis in comparison to patients whose ACE score is 0. Other conditions including heart disease, diabetes, alcoholism, and other types of substance abuse follow the same trend. A male with an ACE score of 6 is 4,600 percent more likely to become an intravenous drug abuser compared to a male with an ACE score of 0. The heroin, according to Felitti's thinking, is not the problem. It's a solution—though crude and ineffective—to blunt internal pain and anguish leftover from a childhood of helplessness and hopelessness.

Now let's take a look at depression. A person with an ACE score of 4 or more is 460 percent more likely to develop depression than someone with a score of 0—and there is a 1,220 percent increase in suicide attempts between the two groups. Extrapolating the Kaiser Permanente data to the general population, Felitti estimates that 75 to 80 percent of all suicide attempts nationally are related to adverse childhood experiences.

It's an eye-opener to realize that the most important determinant of our nation's health is childhood experience. Felitti compares the health problems that appear in adulthood to smoke. The fire that needs to be put out is the high occurrence of adverse childhood experiences that relate so strongly to these health and emotional problems in later life.

I believe that adverse childhood experiences are a factor that predisposes us to burnout not only in our adult years, but also when we're teenagers. Here's an example from my own life.

My First Burnout Experience

I am 16, a junior in high school. Like many people with high ACE scores, I'm already on track for health problems. I smoke and I've just had unprotected sex for the first time. I also have serious migraine headaches, stomach problems, and anxiety. But I'm very smart and scholastically responsible. My French teacher goes on vacation and apparently no substitute can be found, so she asks me to run the class. I'm remarkably good with French idioms and pronunciation, which is why I get a 4 out of 5 on the Advanced Placement (AP) exam after studying the language for a single semester. I've also scored a 5 on the English AP exam and have won an award from the National Council of Teachers of English in my home state of Massachusetts. My parents are proud and frame the letter of congratulations that I get from freshman senator Edward Kennedy.

During this time, I'm also in rehearsal for a play. My role is Ismene, the sister of Antigone, and our drama club is taking part in a state competition. In addition, I've won first place in physics in the science fair for a project that involved growing crystals with lattice defects and then measuring the effect of the defects on the crystals' piezoelectric properties. I'm preparing to exhibit the project in the state finals.

And then, there are boys. The young man who has recently seduced me (he is a senior in a private high school and has started carrying a long umbrella as some sort of presumptive Ivy League affectation) tells me that the signal flags prominently plastered on the door of his Corvette are my initials. My mother intuitively despises "Umbrella Man" and doesn't trust him one bit. She checks out a book on signal flags from the library and—standing by the curb, squinting in the afternoon sun—duly inspects Umbrella Man's car doors. They are *not* my initials. I've been had in the most serious sense of the phrase. He is leaving for Yale in the fall, and despite myself, and the fact that my parents have forbidden me to see him again, I'm crestfallen.

This is the last straw for my sanity.

"Everyone wants a piece of me!" I whine dramatically. "There's nothing left for me." I gave everything to my French teacher, the drama club, the science fair, my parents, and that stupid Umbrella Man who got just what he wanted. My response to all this is to shut the door to my room and refuse to come out. I stay in there for a week, except to visit the bathroom and dining-room table. I am apathetic, withdrawn, disagreeable, and emotionally exhausted.

Am I depressed? No way. At the end of the week, my mother reports that the school has serious concerns about my mental health. Well, that makes me furious. Galvanized by the need to prove myself as invincible and perfect, I return to school and function beautifully.

My soul, however, is roaming untethered in the Land of the Lost, but I continue to go through the motions so well that no one notices that I'm an empty shell. *I* don't even notice until somewhere in my mid-30s. That's when I begin the arduous process of coming back home to myself. In the meantime, I'm hardwired to overachieve, search for perfection, and crash and burn repeatedly.

My childhood experiences, in combination with inborn temperament and external environment, put me at very high risk of burnout. Let's now focus on personality types and makeup, and the ways in which those factors contribute to burnout.

Chapter Four

Personality, Temperament, and Burnout

~~~~~~

"The principle of all successful effort is to try to do not what is absolutely the best, but what is easily within our power, and suited for our temperament and condition."

— JOHN RUSKIN

~~~~~~

A company has downsized, and now all the work has to be done by 60 percent of the staff. Some employees thrive, or at least survive; while others become depressed, withdrawn, hostile, or physically ill. What's the difference between the folks who burn out and the hardier ones who rise to the challenge?

In this chapter, I'll provide you with an overview of some different ways to examine your personality, needs, and temperament; as well as how those factors affect your work situations. My hope is that by understanding yourself better, you'll more often gravitate toward situations that fit your style and avoid ones that go against your grain.

Being a square peg in a round hole doesn't bode well for feeling vital, competent, successful, and at peace with the world. A person who is conflict averse, for example, is much more likely to burn out as a manager than someone who is willing to confront difficult people and situations. Likewise, an individual with an artistic temperament is much more likely to feel alive being a landscape architect than a bookkeeper.

The following pages are packed with fascinating information, so consume them slowly and pay attention to what you learn about yourself. Remember that the journey from the Burnout Inferno through the *Purgatorio* and ultimately to heaven on Earth is one of self-knowledge and inner reflection. When you know how you respond to challenges and have a clear understanding of your unique needs profile, inborn temperament, and personality, you'll bring your best to whatever you do.

The Stress-Hardy Personality

In 1979, psychologist Suzanne Kobasa defined *stress hardiness* based on her study in a corporate setting among Illinois Bell Telephone executives. In a situation of divestiture, when no one knew who would keep their job, who would be transferred, who would be fired, or what the system would look and function like on a daily basis, she discovered an essential difference between the executives who stayed functional and well versus those who stressed out and lost their health.

Kobasa hypothesized that people who were more self-reflective and disciplined in meeting life's challenges might fare better in stressful circumstances. This kind of person understands that change is a natural part of life, that the status quo can't be preserved, and that every life has its inevitable share of challenges and difficulties. They have matured beyond the childhood belief that life is always fair. Thus, it's pointless to blame others and wish that things were different when fairness is nowhere on the horizon and never will be. Authentic control resides in one's own capacity for staying aware of the situation and making the most adaptive choices available with the most auspicious timing. This capacity can also be called *mindfulness*.

The mature individual that Kobasa describes as stress hardy has three essential characteristics. They all begin with the letter *C*, which makes them easy to recall:

1. **Control** is the inclination to believe and act as if you can influence the events of your life. That kind of personal power creates resilience, since even if things aren't going your way, you still believe that you can make things better. The opposite inclination, of course, is helplessness.

People high in the element of control have the capacity to dissect situations and determine *why* things aren't going well without blaming others or the system. *They take responsibility for their own part in whatever is happening* without neurotic self-criticism. A penchant for nonjudgmental self-reflection that optimizes adaptive choice is a good working definition of mindfulness and empowerment. *This capacity—which is damaged in situations that result in learned helplessness—needs to be developed in people prone to burnout.*

2. **Challenge** is based on the understanding that change is the only constant in life. It can, will, and is already and always happening. If you're hanging on to the way things used to be (or are "supposed" to be), you'll eventually have to let go no matter how painful

it is. The essential question regarding change is: *Is it a challenge to evolve or a threat to the status quo?*

Individuals who possess this trait are realists who anticipate stressful events and are therefore more prepared for their occurrence. They're also more likely to instigate change since they're attuned to their environment and know what resources are available (people, technologies, finances, systems, opportunities, and so forth) to create a more functional situation. People high in challenge are natural change navigators. They ride the current of possibility. *People prone to burnout, on the other hand, are more likely to cope through denial and fail to anticipate stressful events.*

3. **Commitment** is based on an inner sense of self-respect that shows up as the willingness to participate meaningfully in every aspect of life, adding value to work, personal relationships, and the community at large. If you're committed to what you do, you stay engaged rather than checking out and becoming alienated, isolated, apathetic, or cynical. This passionate involvement with life supports the deep meaning and solid values at the core of resilience.

In the previous chapter, I mentioned Holocaust survivor and psychiatrist Viktor Frankl in the discussion on learned helplessness and its effects on mental and physical health. Frankl's ability to survive his imprisonment in various concentration camps also provides a perfect example of a committed individual who stayed engaged with life even in the face of seemingly insurmountable difficulties. Inspired by the words of philosopher Friedrich Nietzsche, "That which does not kill me makes me stronger," Frankl continually looked for deeper meaning in the midst of the Holocaust. He was keenly aware of the mind-body connection, observing that those who became helpless and gave up hope died first.

In keeping with his personality, Frankl set his sights on surviving the horrific conditions so that he could teach others how to find meaning even in suffering. *Those of us prone to burnout are more likely to withdraw during challenging situations than stay engaged, and to be deficient in the vital skill of creating meaning.*

Thirty years of research on stress hardiness has confirmed its efficacy in preventing stress, burnout, and illness in groups as diverse as nurses and executives, and radiology technicians and students. *Furthermore, the stress-hardy personality is more than a gift of nature or nurture. It can be learned at any stage of life.*

Kobasa's colleague, psychologist Salvatore Maddi, is a professor at the University of California at Irvine and the founder of the Hardiness Institute, where he created courses to develop an individual's hardiness.[1]

Examining Your Needs and Motivation

If we can learn to be helpless or hardy and make meaning of our experiences, what other types of learning might impact whether or not we're prone to burnout? The work of Dr. David McClelland, the late psychologist and onetime chairman of the Harvard University Department of Social Relations, is central to this question.

McClelland was my mentor for a Medical Foundation Fellowship that I was awarded in 1981 in what was then the nascent field of psychoneuroimmunology. He was in his 60s when I first met him—a strikingly tall and affable man with a white goatee and mustache reminiscent of Colonel Sanders. Always dressed in a jacket and signature bow tie, he had a ready smile and an extremely bright, open, inquiring mind. I think he loved crunching data more than any other human being I've ever known. Learning and research were his passion, which made students like me extremely fortunate to work with him.

Co-founder of McBer (an organizational consulting group)—which is now the McClelland Center within the international consulting firm known as the Hay Group—Dr. McClelland was particularly interested in assessing competency in the workplace. It was a pleasure for him to witness a person with the appropriate abilities performing a job that utilized his or her intrinsic strengths—a win-win situation for all concerned. On the other hand, it was distressing when there was a poor job fit, which resulted not only in an individual's poor work performance, but also in psychological and physiological responses that we would now recognize as burnout.

Father of the field of job-competency assessment and training, McClelland discovered that hiring people based on their academic strengths simply didn't work. Intelligence turns out to matter far less than specific competency in doing a good job. For example, even though I have a high IQ and did well in academic course work, I'm a complete bust at sales. When I'm giving a workshop or lecture, I seem constitutionally unable to mention relevant resources: that I have a Website where future events and training programs are listed, in addition to helpful books and CDs. Were that different, I would have sold enough products by now to be independently wealthy. More sales-savvy colleagues such as Jack Canfield and Mark Victor Hansen of *Chicken Soup for the Soul* fame have an innate competency in this regard.

McClelland's approach to figuring out what is required to do a job well is pretty simple. If you want to know what makes a good shoe salesperson, he explained on our first day together, study the best and worst ones and compare what they do. Maybe the best salesperson is extroverted and friendly, for instance, with a natural tendency to schmooze; while the washout is reserved and quiet. Or perhaps the really great salespeople are the ones who are motivated to excel at whatever they do and pursue their goals relentlessly, while the ineffective salespeople tend to be dreamers.

McClelland believed that our basic motivations stem from needs that are learned because they are rewarded by our family, culture, or social setting. For example, as a child I was rewarded for academic achievement by my family and the larger Jewish immigrant culture of the 1950s. Becoming a doctor, lawyer, dentist, or accountant translated into success in the New World. As a young assistant professor at Tufts Medical School, I was lauded for teaching, attaining funding for research grants, and mentoring medical and dental students. Over time I got better at inspiring my audiences, mastering skills that I'd need later for public speaking. In order to feel at home in my own skin, I still *need* to achieve, inspire, and care for people. These needs are what motivate the way I live and work.

McClelland relied on a psychological instrument called the Thematic Apperception Test (TAT) to determine what a person's "need structure" was like. What types of needs are strongest in comparison to others (this is called a needs profile), and what kinds of careers are a good fit with that profile? Successful leaders, for example, have a high need for socialized power (they are inspiring visionaries) compared to their needs for affiliation (close personal relationships).

The TAT consists of a set of pictures (like a couple on a park bench or a scientist in a laboratory) that you write a story about. McClelland was particularly impressed by the TAT because it's free from the kind of bias that can skew the results of other psychological tests—for example, wanting to please (or mislead) the experimenter, hoping to be socially acceptable, or conforming to your own beliefs about yourself. You can't fool the TAT because you have no idea what the "right" answer is. McClelland compared it to taking a blood sample where different thought types are counted rather than different cell types. These thought types fall into three main categories that translate into the motivations that power behavior:

1. The Need for Achievement (nAch). If you have a high nAch, you're motivated to set challenging goals and will work hard to achieve them. I wanted to obtain a doctorate in biomedical sciences from Harvard, for example, and it took considerable focus and will to pull that off. People with a high nAch are problem solvers who like to excel and take moderate risks because they have the best chance of succeeding. Minimal-risk enterprises aren't very interesting because the payoff is too low; and high-risk goals aren't appealing either, since even if the desired outcome is achieved, the result can feel more like luck than skill.

Individuals high in nAch also require feedback on their performance in order to feel successful. So if your boss (or spouse or lover) doesn't comment on what an outstanding job you've done, you're likely to feel stress, disappointment, or resentment, which contributes to burnout. You do your best work alone or with other high achievers. Can you appreciate how working or living with people who are less interested in achievement than you are might increase your potential for burnout?

2. The Need for Affiliation (nAff). If you're high in the need for affiliation, you might have written a relationship story when presented with the TAT picture of the couple on the park bench. You're motivated to seek out and build loving relationships because fitting in well with other people makes you happy. Those of us high in the need for affiliation are likely to excel in customer-service positions or other venues where direct contact with people is important and valued. My own high nAff explains why I'm so fascinated and involved with giving workshops, running training programs, and building community through social networking.

But high nAff has some spectacular pitfalls, too. If you're overly concerned with maintaining good relations with everyone, you're more likely to conform rather than to question, innovate, or create waves at work or at home. That, of course, can and will come back to haunt you—especially if you know that a certain action is required, but you don't voice it for fear of upsetting or angering people. For a person high in nAff, the need to ensure good relations takes precedence over achievement needs.

The tendency is to make choices that increase popularity rather than doing what's necessary to make a business more productive. That trait has always been true of me: for instance, I schedule clients far apart in case they might need more time than I have allotted; I have difficulty being clear with people who are troublesome in my programs; and, as you've already read, I once had to close a business because two people I loved and respected (who were also principals in the enterprise) didn't get along. When people asked, "How's the business going?" my knee-jerk response was, "It's killing me." And it really was. There was no way to maintain a good relationship among the three of us. The chronic stress of the triangulation fried me to a crisp, and I had to make the difficult choice to close the business.

What I ultimately learned from that burnout episode is that running a business involving other partners is a poor fit for my personality and needs profile.

3. The Need for Power (nPow). Power motivation cuts two ways. Some people have an exaggerated need for personal power over others. These individuals tend to be rude, consume a lot of alcohol, engage in sexual harassment, and collect symbols of power (such as expensive cars, boats, homes, offices, and dependent trophy wives if they are men). *Dependent* is the operative word, since people high in nPow dislike any encroachment upon their authority.

When I first met Dr. McClelland, he was fascinated with what he called the "inhibited power motive syndrome" and its effect on health. When people high in the need for personal power rein themselves in to appear more socially acceptable, their bodies respond negatively to the restraint. Their sympathetic nervous system becomes activated (a stress response), and high blood pressure and heart disease can result.

Situations that require restraint are most likely to lead to burnout for this personality type. They aren't team players; however, as leaders, they are potentially damaging to organizations because they demand personal loyalty rather than creating allegiance to the corporate vision.

The socialized need for power, on the other hand, is the competency most often associated with effective leadership. Rather than being motivated by personal prestige and gain, social power is not an end in itself. It is a means to ensure a socially desirable result that benefits others. People high in social power seek advice from others and are team players who recognize that effective human beings need to have a sense of empowerment and influence over their own jobs, as well as input into the larger system. The socialized-power motive is inspirational and influential, enlisting others in the mission and vision of the organization and empowering them to offer their best.

Dr. McClelland believed that these three major needs are learned through experience and the process of coping with one's environment. Since behavior that gets rewarded increases, needs and motivations develop over time. Managers who are rewarded for achieving company goals, for instance, can learn to take the kind of moderate risks that people who are high in nAch prefer (and which are more likely to pan out). Similarly, a high need for affiliation or social power can be increased when an individual is rewarded for the appropriate behaviors.

For this reason, training programs have been designed to create needs profiles that correlate best with entrepreneurial, managerial, technical, or CEO success.

It turns out, however, that *a person's intrinsic motives can't be decreased; they can only be increased over time.* For me, this means that I'll always have a high need for affiliation, but I can learn how that impacts my work and peace of mind. I know that I have to be particularly mindful of the tendency to put the needs of others above the needs of my organization. Furthermore, someone else negotiates my speaking fees (or I'd probably starve). When a potential client says to my assistant Luzie, "Gee, Joan's fee is a bit high," Luzie has no problem at all explaining why I'm worth every cent.

"So why don't you just go to therapy or take a course in negotiation?" a pragmatic friend once suggested. "You're just too conflict averse, so you let people take advantage of you." That's true. I *am* conflict averse, and I've tried almost every form of therapy known to correct this problem—all to no avail. The zebra cannot change her stripes because they are part and parcel of who she is. Accepting this and honoring my strengths, as well as the limitations inherent in them, has definitely decreased my burnout potential. I'm simply not CEO or managerial material. I am, however, exquisitely attuned to people's inner lives, which makes me particularly competent to write books, such as the one you're reading.

With this short introduction to the theory of needs, even without being tested for your motive profile, you can probably get a sense of whether or not a particular need predisposes you to burnout as it does for me. For more information, go to **www.haygroup.com**. If you type "McClelland Center" into the search window, you can watch videos of David McClelland, as well as Dr. Daniel Goleman, one of his most famous students, who popularized the understanding of Emotional Intelligence (which addresses the ways in which you handle yourself and your relationships).

Inborn Temperament

If you enter **www.humanmetrics.com/cgi-win/ JTypes2.asp** into your Internet browser, you will land on a page called HumanMetrics, where you can take a Jung Typology Test designed by psychologist David Keirsey, the best-selling co-author of *Please Understand Me* and an expert on the assessment of temperament. The test consists of 72 brief questions, which takes approximately ten minutes to complete. When you press the Score It! button, your Myers-Briggs typology, which indicates how you perceive the world and make decisions, will come up in just a few seconds.

The Myers-Briggs Type Indicator was adapted from the theories of psychiatrist Carl Jung as outlined in his book *Psychological Types,* published in the early 1920s. Years later, Katharine Cook Briggs and her daughter, Isabel Briggs Myers, created the inventory hoping that it would help women entering the workforce during World War II find the positions best suited to their temperaments.

Today, the Myers-Briggs inventory is probably the most widely used and well-respected personality test available worldwide. It is based on four dichotomous traits that Jung believed were stable over time, which is the definition of temperament. It's an inborn, immutable way of being in relation to the world around you. Research on twins suggests that these temperamental traits are, to a significant extent, genetically determined. I'll define them as simply as possible:

1. Extroversion versus Introversion (E-I). Extroverts get their juice from interacting with the outside world; introverts, on the other hand, prefer living in their own inner world. Too much external stimulation is exhausting for introverts, but extroverts are happiest when connecting with others.

2. Intuition versus Sensation (N-S). Intuitives (N) tend to see the big picture and get their information in a more right-brained way that recognizes patterns and intuits the flow of events. In past years, they might have been thought of as flaky, but today, intuition is a trait sought out by many corporations since "gut knowing" is central to success. Sensing persons, in contrast, use their five senses to appraise the world and gather information from what they see, hear, feel, touch, and taste. They are more concrete, black-and-white thinkers who perceive events and people as individual data points rather than interconnected energies.

3. Thinking versus Feeling (T-F). Thinking people make decisions based on data and observable facts. It's not very romantic, but it works quite well for engineers and scientists. There is definitely a gender sorting that takes place in this dimension. More men are thinking types, while more women are feeling types who make decisions based on those feelings.

4. Perception versus Judgment (P-J). This dichotomy wasn't originally posited by Jung, but was added later by Meyers and Briggs. Perceiving people tend to be spontaneous and go with the flow. They're a lot of fun, but they don't always get things done in an orderly manner. On the other hand, judging people are more likely to be neat, timely, organized, responsible, practical, and good at meeting deadlines.

Those eight possible temperaments combine to form 16 personality profiles: ISTJ, ISFJ, INFJ, INTJ, ISTP, ISFP, INFP, INTP, ESTP, ESFP, ENFP, ENTP, ESTJ, ESFJ, ENFJ, and ENTJ. In my experience, these profiles are dead-on descriptors of how a person perceives reality and navigates the world. I, for example, am an ENFJ—the archetypal Teacher, which is a subset of the idealist temperament (we'll discuss those subsets next).

David Keirsey distills these 16 personality types into four basic temperament groupings—idealists, rationals, artisans, and guardians—that vary in patterns of communication, actions, values, talents, and attitudes. More than 40 million people have used his temperament assessment, which is employed by the U.S. Army, IBM, Yale University, the Fuller Theological Seminary, Pfizer, Shell, Motorola, Charles Schwab, and many other Fortune 500 companies. Here are brief descriptions of the four temperament groupings:[2]

1. Idealists (NFs), which make up 15 to 20 percent of the population, share the following core characteristics:

> Idealists are enthusiastic, they trust their intuition, yearn for romance, seek their true self, prize meaningful relationships, and dream of attaining wisdom.

Idealists pride themselves on being loving, kind-hearted, and authentic.

Idealists tend to be giving, trusting, spiritual, and they are focused on personal journeys and human potentials.

Idealists make intense mates, nurturing parents, and inspirational leaders.[3]

These descriptions fit me to a T. Keirsey delineates four categories of idealists: the Teacher, Champion, Healer, and Counselor. As I mentioned, I'm a Teacher. This type excels in bringing forth the potential of their students, is warm and outgoing, and is, according to Keirsey —this specificity amazed me—"remarkably good with language, especially when communicating in speech, face to face." Teachers, Keirsey concludes, can become charismatic public speakers, which is probably my greatest talent and competency.

Being nailed with surgical precision is a fascinating experience. As you read about the other three temperament groups, which one do you resonate with? (Be sure to go to Keirsey's Website [**www.keirsey.com**] and take the test. When you know your type, read about how it affects everything from your love life to your career.)

2. Artisans (SPs), 30 to 35 percent of the population, are just what you might imagine. They enjoy working with their hands and creating things you can see and touch. Artisans are upbeat, fun loving, spontaneous, and often charming. Impulsive, unconventional, and freewheeling, they are extroverted and enthusiastic. They live for the joys of the day. Artisans fall into four categories: Crafter, Performer, Promoter, and Composer. A career behind a desk crunching numbers would most likely create burnout in artisans—that is, if they stayed at such a job too long.

3. Guardians (SJs), 40 to 45 percent of the population, are the pillars of society. They're kind, loyal, dependable, practical, and hardworking. Highly responsible, concerned citizens, they abide by the rules, uphold traditions, support authority, and build community. They fall into four archetypal categories: Protector, Supervisor, Provider, and Inspector.

4. Rationals (NTs), 5 to 10 percent of the population, are autonomous, scientifically minded, pragmatic skeptics oriented toward problem solving. According to Keirsey, they pride themselves on being "ingenious, independent, and strong willed." Keirsey further characterizes Rationals as even-tempered people who "trust logic, yearn for achievement, seek knowledge, prize technology, and dream of understanding how the world works." Once they put their mind to a problem, they'll work tirelessly to achieve a solution. Rationals are made up of four categories: Architect, Field Marshal, Inventor, and Mastermind.

The "Big Five" Personality Factors

Just as Jung, Myers, and Briggs defined temperament in terms of dichotomous traits, so did several personality theorists who came after them. American psychologist Gordon Allport combed the dictionary for adjectives used to describe personality and then factored them into clusters that were subsequently whittled down to extroversion versus introversion, emotional stability versus neuroticism, openness versus closed-mindedness, agreeableness versus hostility, and conscientiousness versus unreliability. These are known as the "Big Five" personality factors, and several of them have been linked either positively or negatively to burnout.

When I posted an inquiry on Facebook asking *why* people burn out, one woman cited enthusiasm as a prime contender. Burnout is a particular affliction of the enthusiastic, she reasoned. If there's no fire to begin with, then there's nothing to burn out.

Her hypothesis sounds reasonable, but research proves otherwise. Enthusiasm is negatively related to emotional exhaustion, a statistic that makes sense since extroverts are constitutionally self-confident, active, optimistic, and prone to seeking excitement. More emotionally positive than introverts, they tend to look for the benefits in problems and have a lot of enthusiasm, defined as a kind of innate "dispositional energy."

Enthusiastic individuals are more resilient in the face of stress and even disaster. I asked Bob Stilger, a friend of mine who does community-building work in Africa, what enables so many African women—who have been raped, have witnessed family members die, or have lost everything—to pick themselves up and go on. Bob described a kind of energy and vigor that kept the women focused on creating a better future. Rather than folding up inside their misery, they reached out to one another and kept fanning the fires of the possible.

Although enthusiasm is a genetic endowment, researchers in resilience and mind-body medicine are interested in whether it can also be acquired through learning. Hopefully so, as it has been linked to improved physical *and* mental health. Benjamin Chapman, Ph.D., assistant professor of psychiatry at the University of Rochester Medical Center, was the lead author of a 2009 study that linked the "dispositional energy" component of extroversion to dramatically lower levels of interleukin-6 (IL-6), a stress-related immune factor that causes the kind of "bad" inflammation that predisposes individuals to illness. Low levels of extroversion in aging women, the researchers discovered, may lead to an increase in IL-6, which has been linked to a doubling of the risk of death within five years. That data will encourage me to go to more parties and collaborate on new projects!

If extroversion and enthusiasm are good for you, the personality factor known as *neuroticism* is a disaster. Jenny Kim, associate professor at Washington State University School of Hospitality Business Management, linked neuroticism and burnout in people who worked in a fast-food chain. The neurotics among us are chronically and enduringly negative and easily overwhelmed by stress. They tend to have low self-esteem and be fearful, helpless, angry, guilty, and depressed. Neurotics (and I come from a long line of them) set unrealistically high goals, underestimate their performance, and then engage in merciless self-flagellation. Can this personality factor be changed? I'm sure of it, since I'm living proof. The key is to recognize it in yourself, identify it when it's happening, and ask yourself if there is some other way to respond to the situation.

Here's an example: Roger is the kind of person who gets elated over positive feedback and despondent over negative feedback or—and this is key—*no* feedback. No feedback creates a vacuum in which his neurotic mind can spin imaginative scenarios of rejection, failure, and incompetence. Roger compares himself to others, beats himself up for being inferior, and then searches his past for the source of his failure: His school was lousy. His father was abusive. His mother worked. His younger sister got all the glory. What can a guy do when he's dealt such a lousy hand?

So what *is* Roger supposed to do?

— **Recognize his neurotic thinking pattern.** A neurotic thinking pattern is negative, self-critical, hopeless, helpless, and blaming. Getting stuck in it leads to the same stale place over and over again: depression and burnout. Since the recognition of this pattern is a step toward freedom, Roger can feel relief, hope, and a certain sense of heroism when he catches himself floating down the same old mental river: *Whew, I just caught my neurotic thinking . . . amazing how clear it is. Now I can work on changing it. That's awesome!*

— **Release tension.** Thinking patterns are also physical patterns, and if physical patterns aren't changed, they will hook you right back into the familiar thinking patterns with which they're associated. Try this experiment: Close your eyes and remember a time when you were trapped in negative thinking (like Roger's experience). Perhaps you were thinking about why you failed at love or work and what that might mean to your future.

Now notice how your body responded to those thoughts. Where is the tension? Are you holding your breath, or is your breathing shallow and ragged? Next, blow out your breath with a big sigh, and relax your shoulders. On the next in-breath, imagine that you can take the air into your belly. When you exhale, let your belly flatten and feel your whole body relax, from head to toe. Take ten belly breaths, continuing to relax a little bit more on each exhalation. Physical release changes the brain and sets up the conditions for thinking differently.

— **Consider an alternative.** What kind of thoughts would support the spacious, relaxed feeling you got from belly breathing? The stress-hardy thinking of an emotionally mature person should do the trick. So Roger recalls the three C's: *control, challenge,* and *commitment.* He is specific and thinks about how he can feel some control over the situation that he's obsessing about, what life challenge he's meeting, and how meaningful the process is that he's engaged with.

— **Engage in self-recognition.** Roger gives himself a thumbs-up, the kind of positive feedback he needs to change his thinking patterns.

Thinking patterns take time to change, but they are malleable. The brain and nervous system continue to make new connections throughout life, a process known as *neuroplasticity.* We can actually develop new neural pathways that modify our perceptions, thoughts, and behaviors.

Thoughts are like drops of water that coalesce into streams that deepen over time as more water carves the course. But even when the water starts to flow in a different direction and a new stream forms, the old channel still remains. It may be months or years before thoughts start to flow automatically in the new channel. I still catch my own neurotic thinking from time to time.

Knowledge Is Power

There are an infinite number of ways to appreciate the differences that make us human. Some of us are enthusiastic optimists, and others are congenitally neurotic pessimists. There are people who need people and Svengalis who need power. There are high-achieving go-getters and laid-back philosophers.

You can study personality with a variety of systems that are fascinating windows on what shapes your unique personality, temperament, and worldview. But the bottom line is this: *If you know who you are and accept it, then you're less likely to waste energy trying to be something you're not.* It's the struggle that will burn you out. And it's the acceptance of who you are that lets you relax and soften your edges. The result is the natural joy of living comfortably in your own skin.

Once you get comfortable with who you are, the next challenge is to maintain your autonomy by being selective about the people you allow into your life (or keep out) and how you utilize your energy. In the next chapter, you'll learn how to cultivate the fine art of energy management by paying attention to your boundaries.

Chapter Five

Energy Management

"A shamanic practitioner I worked with once said, 'Learn and live by your own body's rhythm.' Simple, but it profoundly affected me by making me aware of what my body needs and understanding what it is and isn't capable of. If we don't learn to manage our energy ourselves, there will be plenty of people, projects, and events that will do it for us. And no one will ever be wiser about our needs than we are."

— FACEBOOK FRIEND MICHELE LAWSON

During the worst relationship of my life (I'll spare you the gruesome details), I broke out in a strange rash that covered my abdomen, buttocks, and thighs. "Dry skin," the first dermatologist remarked, but lotion wasn't the cure. A second dermatologist surveyed the rash with concern and sent her assistant to fetch a biopsy kit. She was worried that the rash might be a lymphoma, but it proved to be a noncancerous infiltrate of lymphocytes (immune cells) into my skin. Typically an ailment that afflicts adolescent males and clears up in a few weeks, my case was chronic and persisted for more than two years. I was an outlier in the annals of dermatology—a cover girl for the odd.

My doctor wanted to start me on chemotherapy. Even though the condition wasn't cancerous, there didn't seem to be any other way to clear up the persistent rash. I declined since the potential cure seemed altogether worse than the disease. Fascinated with mind-body medicine, I was more interested in the person with the illness than the disease itself. How were these rough red blotches related to the story of my life?

My ill-chosen lover came directly to mind. He was a person of great promise in many regards, but also someone of monumental brokenness. Ever idealistic—my assistant, Luzie, calls me an innocent—I hoped that my sweet, sweet love would save him. I apparently missed my true calling as a country singer. *Light enters at the broken places* was my mantra.

The trouble was that because I was so fixated on *him,* I couldn't see my own brokenness. I've had a life-long tendency to indiscriminately offer up my jugular vein to all comers, and the result has often been nothing short of a disastrous loss of energy culminating in burnout. Rather than protecting myself and setting limits, I had allowed my boyfriend (who was the latest manifestation of my pathological idealism) to invade every aspect of my life. By doing so, my health, finances, friendships, work, and peace of mind all took a huge hit. Had I paid more attention to what my body was trying to tell me through the rash, I might have bailed on the toxic relationship sooner, but idealists often stay in bad situations too long, hoping for a miracle.

You can view your immune system as a kind of internal militia that keeps invaders from taking over. It manufactures antibodies that prevent bacteria, viruses, and fungi from colonizing your body and sucking the life out of you. An inflammatory response (like the rash on my skin) is the body's way of setting a strong boundary to keep itself intact. Your skin is your other source of protection. It's a physical barrier that separates you from the rest of the world. Think about it. Without skin, it would be impossible to take a bath or get dressed! You'd just leak all over the place.

So my illness was a double-barreled metaphor involving two boundary organs—the immune system and skin. It was perfect for getting the attention of someone as dense and headstrong as I can be. I had succumbed to a near deadly invasion by a person whom I had willingly allowed to drain my life-force energy. This was a bitter pill to swallow, since I don't buy the oversimplified view that illnesses always convey a deeper symbolic meaning about the self. But this one surely did, at least for me.

The combination of idealism, weak boundaries, and helper's disease ("I can save him!") is like nitroglycerin. It has the potential not only to burn you out . . . but worse still, to blow you up. When I could finally admit that I'd given all of my energy to a human vampire, I left the relationship. Within two months of acting on my body's wisdom and taking back my power (as well as my life), the rash disappeared for good.

FBF Betsy Mullen shared some powerful advice she received on this topic from her dear friend and mentor Antoinette Spurrier:

> A lot of times, if we believe we're moving toward a greater vision, we also feel that we can be the sacrificial lamb. But if we allow

our spirit—our spiritual core—to get violated repeatedly without standing up for ourselves, we are in a place of not acting in merit toward our own spiritual nature. When we look at our desire to help others, maybe too much of our power gets transferred. In the desire to bring forward the higher goal, perhaps there are levels of repeated violations that we allow, because we have transferred our authority. But what is the greater spiritual good if we violate our own wellness at a physical, psychological, emotional, and spiritual level?

Ironically, "self-violation" is common both in health-care providers and among the clergy. FBF Teri Gilmore wrote the following:

> As a clergyperson, I can attest to many cases of burnout in the priesthood. Much of it comes from inappropriate boundaries—not knowing how to set limits on time when we are available to parishioners (that is what caller ID and message machines are for), not taking two whole days off each week, not taking long enough vacations, and trying to be everything to everyone.

There's a lot of talk about balancing our own needs with the needs of others. But without a vision that transcends the polarity between maintaining strong boundaries and offering help to others, the road to balance is hard to find. However, Kabbalism—the ancient mystical teaching of the Zohar (the classic text of Jewish mysticism)—has just such a vision.

Creating a "Beautiful Synthesis"

First let me offer a very short course on the Kabbalistic "Tree of Life," which is no less than the software program for Creation. (Whether or not this jibes with the creation story you prefer, just consider the following as a metaphor that can help you understand how to balance your own energy system.)

I remember lying in bed as a child and wondering how something—how *everything*—could have possibly arose from nothing. Fortunately, Kabbalah offers an answer to that intriguing question. Here is a summary of how that happens.

The Tree of Life comprises ten luminous globes of energy (light) called the *sephiroth,* and each individual *sephira* is a Divine attribute—a pattern of energy—through which God creates the continuously evolving universe. The sephiroth are in dynamic interaction within and between four interconnected Trees of Life, which manifest four worlds of creation, from the most subtle to our densest material world. These worlds correspond roughly to the human mind, soul, heart (emotions), and body.

At the top of the tree sits the first sephira, known as *Keter*—"the Crown." It represents the will of the Absolute to step out of itself in the form of a Creator that emanates the seen and unseen universes. That is how something appears out of nothing.

Sephiroth two through seven (from right to left down the Tree of Life, excluding the one labeled *Da'at*) form pairs of opposites. For example, the fourth sephira *Hesed,* which means loving-kindness, is balanced by *Gevurah*, the fifth sephira meaning strength or boundaries. These two opposing principles combine (similar to the Taoist yin and yang) and give rise to the sixth sephira called *Tif'eret,* which is the emanation of the Divine Will as beauty, balance, and harmony.

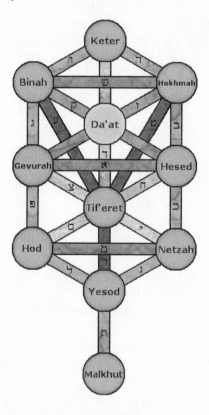

The Kabbalistic Tree of Life illustrating the ten sephiroth. (The lighter colored sphere labeled *Da'at* is a subconscious mirror of *Keter* and isn't counted.)[1]

Rabbi Shimon Leiberman, writing for the Jewish Website **www.aish.com**, describes how the balance of *Hesed* and *Gevurah* creates the transcendent energy of *Tif'eret,* which he calls a "beautiful synthesis." His understanding sheds light on how we can manage the urge to tend, befriend, rescue, and help with the need to maintain our own boundaries in a way that encourages others to find and mobilize their own strengths.

Leiberman uses the example of a democracy whose leader has to ensure the survival of the nation. To that end, there's a state department (*Hesed,* sometimes spelled *"Chesed"*) whose job is to cultivate good relations among nations. There's also a department of defense (*Gevurah*) whose job is to prepare for war. The essential goals and philosophies of these two departments are completely at odds.

How can they be reconciled? Is there a worldview that includes yet transcends these disparate positions? A broader perspective—to ensure economic and human development while keeping its citizens safe and boundaries intact—is provided by the vision of the nation's leader. Sometimes military might is the necessary strategy, while at other times, it is friendship and understanding. Wisdom lies in knowing when to use each, without adopting either one as a sole ideology. Leiberman explains:

> *Chesed* [*Hesed*] has an innate "ideology" of goodness. It wants to give for the sake of giving. It sees in this the ultimate goal, and the more one gives—regardless who is deserving—the greater and better things.
>
> *Gevurah,* on the other hand, sees giving as poisonous. Only things earned by equal and fair labor are "good." Thus, it has a powerful ideology

of "quid pro quo" and "no free lunches." It sees the ultimate goal of creation as every creature earning its own way.

Tif'eret comes along creating a synthesis of both of these approaches. It includes both of these approaches because it has a broader goal in mind, and therefore makes use of both. Its goal is "the development of the human being to his greatest potential."[2]

Extending the metaphor to our own lives, if we constantly push ourselves to do more, serve more, love more, and give more, the ideology of *Hesed* will cause us to burn out. That's exactly what happens to many idealistic people who work in the human-services sector. Learning how to take care of oneself is indeed an art—one that I've addressed in my books *Inner Peace for Busy People* and *Inner Peace for Busy Women*.

We also need to know when, how, and under what circumstances to mobilize *Gevurah*. When I was writing this book, for instance, I needed to establish very strict boundaries so that I could carve out blocks of uninterrupted time. If you e-mailed me during this period, you would have received this autoreply: "I am either traveling or on retreat meeting a pressing book deadline. No matter who you are and how much I love you, I am unavailable for e-mail, visits, or phone calls until mid-February. No exceptions! Contact my assistant, Luzie, at . . ."

FBF Lauren Rosenfeld, also a student of Kabbalah, made an insightful point about *Gevurah* as *discernment*— the art of sensing which activities, tasks, or people to let in (or keep out of) your life at any given time so that you can live in the most inspired way.

Lauren posted this during our discussion:

> We tend to think about Divine inspiration as an unbridled outpouring of Divine light. But sometimes, it comes in the form of *discernment:* the wisdom and strength to intuitively know what we will allow in and what we have the strength to turn away. In Kabbalah, *Gevurah*—strength/limitation/judgment—is indeed a Divine energy. We can get in touch with the Divine power of discernment and know what we should limit in our lives.

Coming to Balance

Knowing what to limit in your life and what to seek more of isn't always easy to figure out, let alone implement. The tendency for all idealists—and for most women, whether idealistic or not—is to give selflessly until they drop.

Bob Mason, a friend of mine who has devoted years to learning the ways of the Pueblo Indians, once returned from a ceremonial dance and told me about an insight he received during a "giveaway." (A giveaway is a ceremony where you place a treasured belonging on a blanket for someone else to have. You, too, can then take something that you need, so the ceremony is reciprocal, and all participants are helped.) Bob heard an inner voice during the giveaway that simply said, *Do not place yourself on the giveaway blanket because you are not yours to give.*

When you give away what isn't yours in the first place—the vitality of your soul—you're engaging in an act of self-sabotage. Your generosity, while it may appear selfless on the surface, is really selfish in that it serves the ego (the desire to be right, look good, feel accepted, be rewarded, feel holy, and so forth) rather than the soul's purpose, which is uniquely yours. Serving the ego is draining, but serving the soul is energizing.

FBF Gina Vance wrote:

> It is helpful to ask whom we serve and why, especially on less-than-conscious levels of awareness. For that which drives us to extinguishment may be something like: "If only I give enough to this idealized God figure I am serving and sacrificing for, then I will someday be returned the favor [ultimately love]."

Love is always the answer. But the question is how to honor and love ourselves so that our actions serve the soul. The soul cooperates with the Tree of Life—that larger field of creative energy. The ego, on the other hand, is powered by our own limited adrenal energy that eventually burns out. Paying attention to our energy, and how various acts affect it, is instrumental in learning how to discern where right boundaries are at any moment.

FBF Sheila Weidendorf wrote:

> Limits can be liberating—meaning that we can't do everything, every day, all the time. If *no* doesn't really mean no, then *yes* is meaningless as well. A little self-awareness and the willingness to set boundaries can go a long, long way in maintaining balance in work and life.
>
> Determine where the world's needs and

your own personal skill and joy intersect, and then put your apples in that basket. Be clear about what you can and cannot offer, and respect your own boundaries so that others will respect them, too. Then work is joyful, balance is a foundational principle, and there's less there to cause burnout.

Sheila offers a very clear definition of self-love, which I think of as a Divine attribute that resides within each of us. Another vital aspect of this is asking for help. FBF Joe Buchman described how this has impacted his life:

Taking care of a terminally ill spouse can be overwhelming. Burnout seemed to creep up on me overnight. I had to force myself to slow down and take a break, and realize that everything doesn't have to be perfect. I've also learned to accept help. I have a bag of "emotional tools" I use: I manage my stress with healthy eating, yoga, and meditation; and I try to get a good night's sleep each night. I'm so grateful to my brother who gives me the time to put those tools to good use.

FBF Lauren Rosenfeld agreed, saying:

For me, the antidote to burning out is reaching out. When I'm feeling burned out, it's usually a result of my belief that I can do it alone . . . that I can handle it all myself. When burnout hits, I want to retreat, which is more of the same, isn't it? *I can do it all by myself; I can recover by myself.* And so I reach out. I allow others to do for me, to support me, to enfold me. To make me tea or make me laugh. "I am who I am because of who you are," says the wise, laughing heart. And it is with a wise and laughing heart—a heart that listens to and rejoices with others—that I reemerge renewed.

"If only the world I work in would catch up with this level of consciousness," commented FBF Lavinia Gene Weissman during our wonderful conversation on boundaries and self-love. The next chapter deals with what to do when your workplace doesn't understand the conversation, and it's time to let go and move on.

Chapter 6

Letting Go
and Moving On

~~~~~~

*"I've changed careers when my
interests changed and passion left. To overcome
burnout, I followed my passion to where it went next."*

— FACEBOOK FRIEND **VALERIE SIEGEL**

~~~~~~

Gone are the days when most people kept the same career from "cradle to grave" and then retired with a pension.

I did have that opportunity as an academic, educating medical and dental students as well as doing cancer research. But then my passion moved elsewhere. In the late 1970s, my father chose to end his life by jumping out a window when medical treatment for his leukemia caused a serious and destructive mania that was never addressed by his physicians. The treatment was keeping the cancer in check, so they said, but his soul had already fled. Dad's death changed the course of my life. My passion shifted from unlocking the secrets of cancer cells in the laboratory to helping people with cancer (and their families) make a safe passage through the alien territory of illness.

I retrained as a clinical psychologist and moved from Tufts Medical School back to Harvard Medical

School to create mind-body programs that empowered patients to find meaning in their challenges, let go of the past, and stay open to the future with all its hope and uncertainty. Since then, I've also become an author, public speaker, spiritual guide, radio-show host, and journalist. Some of these transitions have been organic and gradual; and other changes have been much less graceful, requiring the equivalent of a crowbar to enable me to let go and move on.

This chapter is about finding *your* courage when it's time to create a future different from your past. The first step is to recall what your inner spark feels like. Your passion—your life energy—is the fuel that moves you from the inertia of being fried to the excitement of the life that is emerging for you in the here-and-now.

Recalling the Energy of Passion

Passion is pure energy—vitality—which is exactly what dies in burnout. When you've lost the spark of vitality that animates you, it's hard to remember what passion feels like, so let me remind you with a story.

Gordon and I were celebrating New Year's Eve with our friends Chris and Dave Hibbard at the historic Gold Hill Inn, which is in the tiny mining town where we live high in the foothills of Boulder, Colorado. The Inn, as we locals call it, is an impressive log saloon decorated with authentic memorabilia left over from the brief gold rush in the late 1800s. The mood was festive, with roaring fires in the three huge fireplaces and revelers dressed in a fantastic array of mountain chic. Sequined evening dresses with cowboy boots, jeans, and vintage hats added that *je ne sais quoi* mountain character to the celebration.

Heidi and the Rhythm Rollers provided the early-evening entertainment. The band boasted a bass player, guitarist, and drummer. The magnificent young Heidi was all dolled up in a red taffeta dress from the '50s, a pair of vintage black five-inch heels with ankle straps, long red earrings, and a white tieback for her long copper hair. And she could sing.

A dark-haired boy about six years old planted himself directly in front of her and began to dance his heart out. He danced alone and he danced with whoever came along, entirely unself-conscious and grooving on the music. He was a riveting show all by himself.

"I think he has a crush on Heidi," his mother offered as she passed by our table. And sure enough, when the vivacious singer finally took a break while the band kept playing, the little boy marched right over and asked her to dance. He was clearly in heaven, having followed his passion to its six-year-old pinnacle—a dance with the mythical goddess in the shiny red dress.

Take a few moments to ponder these questions: *When was the last time you felt so much enthusiasm and joy that you could dance for hours—literally or metaphorically? Do you still feel passion in your work? Even if it has dissipated, can you find a spark worth fanning? Or do you think it's time to move on?*

FBF Theresa DaKay wrote this about maintaining your passion:

> I had to move my Circles of Grace program
> to another population to avoid burnout and

reignite my enthusiasm. Divine inspiration led me to community mental health for three years, but to save myself, and so I could help others, I had to move on, knowing that the seeds I planted would be germinated in their own time—or rather, in the Divine's time. I moved into a university setting, where my enthusiasm is aided by the energy of the youth. As the poet David Whyte would say, *I was not leaving, but rather, arriving.* You don't go away from so much as you go forward, moving within and through your own circles of grace.

Theresa knew what her passion was and found a way to fan the flame of enthusiasm for it in a new setting. Change requires courage, which can be hard to muster. In my clinical and personal experience, I've found that most of us know when it's time to leave a job or relationship long before we actually make the leap.

The Anatomy of Change

FBF Christina McDowell wrote:

I think one of the biggest life lessons we all have to learn (and I speak from experience and in seeing this in many of my clients), is in knowing and trusting that inner voice that says, *Darlin', it's time to cut and run.* It implies forward movement, and the fear of an unknown future then looms. And sometimes, that monster of the unknown can be so large that we choose to stay, because the devil we know is better than the devil we don't know.

Reaching out and receiving support for what we are afraid of allows us to release the energy blocks and fears that are holding us back, and gives us the renewed breath to move into a more fulfilling, intentionally designed future. Even if nothing changes on the physical plane, just beginning this process emotionally is enough to relieve burnout.

The process of letting go and moving on that Christina describes is both enlivening and terrifying. What if you decide to leave a relationship but you can't pay the rent on your own? What if you finally quit a job that's burning you out and end up as a statistic in the annals of unemployment? It takes courage to walk away from a bird in the hand to catch a more beautiful one that's still in the bush. But this familiar tension is the plot that animates the best of adventures.

The most successful Hollywood epics are based on what happens when the hero makes a leap (or is pushed) into the unknown. Anthropologists refer to this letting go of the old as a *rite of passage*. It consists of three parts: the hero separates from his or her former life, confronts ordeals in the intermediate time between "no longer and not yet," and finally enters the "promised land" of a new life transformed by the adventure.

The late, great mythologist Joseph Campbell called this evolutionary leap the *hero's journey*. But the three-part anatomy of change and transformation isn't limited to epic stories. It's the map of soul growth for all of us, lived out in the more familiar contexts of love and work.

Consider Meryl Streep's character, Jane Adler, in the 2009 film *It's Complicated*. Jane's 20-year marriage ends when she's dumped for a younger woman (*separation from the old life*), which pushes her into the second stage of the journey, *the liminal time between no longer and not yet*. By the end of the film (having faced the ordeals of living on her own, discovering her passion in work, and coming to grips with her ex who suddenly wants her back), Jane has blossomed and enters the final stage of the journey: *transformation and empowerment*.

Transformation—a deepening into one's authentic nature—is what burnout ultimately demands. Just as an acorn has an entelechy (an inner blueprint that expresses itself as an oak tree), each one of us has an inner essence that we mature into. That essence is expressed by following our passion, our deepest longing, our bliss.

"Follow your bliss," Joseph Campbell insisted, which inspired an entire generation of spiritual seekers. That sounds easy enough, but actually pulling it off requires courage, trust, and faith. There are dragons to slay before you can claim the future that has been searching for you all along. There is no map for the journey, and trusting the GPS inside you takes chutzpah.

When my husband, Gordon, and I wrote *Your Soul's Compass*, we interviewed 27 sages from different wisdom traditions, trying to get some idea of how to listen to that inner direction finder. One of the sages we spoke to was Episcopal priest Reverend Dr. Cynthia Bourgeault, who is among the greatest female wisdom teachers of our time. When we asked Reverend Cynthia how to listen for inner guidance, she focused on two areas: paying exquisite attention to the cues that life provides and trusting the unknown. She compared the latter to making a leap of faith, intuitively knowing that you're not diving into an empty swimming pool.

Trust and Faith

When I give workshops on burnout, participants' personal inquiries into trust and faith are always a highlight, filled with big "Aha!" moments that can help them better understand their fear and courage.

We explore the topic in a structured exercise. People sit together in groups of three, strangers willing to open up to themselves and each other. Each person is given ten minutes of uninterrupted time to talk about what trust and faith mean to him or her. While one person speaks, another group member listens attentively with eyes open (and mouth shut); and the last member listens with closed eyes, holding the speaker and listener consciously in his or her awareness. The opportunity to speak without interruption, and to be received without judgment, is rare. The kindness of an attentive listener opens up space for unexpected insights to arise.

When everyone has taken a turn in each role, the three members of the group then discuss their experience. This is usually accompanied by laughter, tears, and leaning in close to each other to harvest the nectar of every word and gesture.

The Facebook gang chewed on inquiries about trust and faith in a less structured way over several months and taught me quite a bit about the inner mechanics of letting go.

"Faith is rooted in the Unknown," posted FBF David Jon Peckinpaugh. "It can't be established on the basis of any belief—whether positive or negative. If it is, then it's not faith . . . it's something else."

David is the delightful author of two books, including *Buddha & Shakespeare: Eastern Dharma, Western Drama.* He is a wise and witty popular blogger (a wit he used well when he came up with *Fried* as a title for this book). This intrepid and outspoken friend named one of the core competencies for spiritual maturity: *comfort with or at least tolerance for the unknown.*

FBF Susan Saharko Hartman equated *trust* with *hope:*

I have come to learn through some very tough life lessons that absolutely nothing in life stays the same. Everything changes, whether I like it or not. Once I was able to wrap my emotions around this, I found hope. And hope showed me the gift of curiosity and wonderment of what just might be waiting around the corner for me. Hope has become my beacon to let go of the need for certainty and truly live my life.

FBF Gloria Byrom Agrelius responded:

I love the word *hope.* It feels like a prayerful and generous heart sharing love. A hopeful heart is a knowing heart that holds us to greater potentiality. When we face and embrace all that is before us, we allow unconditional love to be the energy of change. It is our own resistance that feeds the energy we no longer wish to experience.

FBF Sweigh Emily Spilkin added the following:

Basic trust—when I can lean back into it—
reminds me that there's something larger than
me that's holding it all . . . it's not all up to me, and
"it" (life) isn't what it appears to be. Basic trust
is a net or matrix, a connection to the context
of goodness that's all around us, but sometimes
difficult to see. Faith is the leap that I must make
from the way the material world (pain, suffering,
feeling overwhelmed) sometimes appears to that
larger matrix of goodness. Even when I can't feel
it (or especially when I can't feel it), faith is the
vehicle that gets me there.

And FBF Yvonne Roza also commented, saying:

The energy of faith and trust is like a sacred
pause for me when I can take a long, deep,
conscious breath of remembrance. Remembering
who I truly am, the bigger picture, the Divine
bottom line. But this could not be without having
taken a few turns around the burnout bend.

FBF Mary-Lynne Monroe posted this bit of wisdom
from Nobel Prize–winning author André Gide: "One
does not discover new lands without consenting to lose
sight of the shore for a very long time." She continued
in her own voice, saying, "We can't have new experiences or be reborn without letting go of the past, of
what we know, and sometimes even who we know and
who we are."

Letting go of anything, no matter what it is, brings you to the same place—the present moment where there is nothing to resist and nothing to defend. It is what it is, and all you can do is embrace the Now. One line from *A Course in Miracles* has always remained with me: "In my defenselessness, my safety lies." Without an ego agenda that keeps you tethered to specific space/time coordinates, you are indeed guided by what I call the Great Triad of Becoming—love, harmony, and beauty.

Whether you're doing your familiar job, looking for a new one, playing with your kids, or out walking the fields, you do it with more grace, elegance, and joy. This is the great revival that burnout can lead you to.

Chapter Seven

The Great Revival—
Awakening in the Now

*"If you want to get back to the garden,
you have to become a gardener."*

— My husband, **Gordon Dveirin**

It's the Fourth of July, and this manuscript is due to my publisher the day after tomorrow. But I just can't work toward a deadline in the same frenzied way that I used to. Gordon and I have spent much of the morning wandering in the mountains with our dogs and admiring the gardens we've put so much effort into this season. From time to time, I come inside, sit down at the computer, and write. The process feels natural, without any of the unpleasant aftertaste of burned adrenal energy.

By the midafternoon, Gordie and I walk the five mountain acres where we live with Milo, our standard poodle puppy; and Sophie, our wise old Aussie who has taken him in so generously. It's raining big warm drops as we visit half a dozen different ecosystems on the land and exclaim over every last wildflower and blade of grass. The ability of nature to revitalize and adapt to changing circumstances is nothing short of breathtaking.

Gordie looks at me and smiles as we make our way back to the house, hand in hand, so I can return to writing. He's exuberant that I've come back to life. With my revival, our relationship also feels fresh and exciting. Burnout, after all, is a family affair.

In part, by tending to our gardens, we have also been nurturing a renewed relationship with life and each other. "The lure of the garden has been like falling in love all over again," Gordie remarks. "That's what you've been doing these last months, Joanie. It's been an incredible time of renewal. A rite of spring *and* a rite of passage. Our gardening here—our practice—has created a seamless transition between nature's own beauty and what we're able to add to it. To be a gardener is to enter into a whole different relationship with nature. That's the secret of beauty. To arrive at harmony between ourselves and what grows all around us. The healing of our souls depends upon this, and in the process, we enter a dance with life that fosters abundance, generosity of spirit, deep appreciation, and the full joy of aliveness."

The Great Revival into Wholeness

The gift of burnout, as Gordie so beautifully expressed it, is a healing into the full joy of aliveness. That healing, a return to what author and educator Parker Palmer calls "the hidden wholeness," is a revelation that's right under our collective noses.

One of the great delights in writing this book so publicly on Facebook was that the FBFs bore witness to, and participated in, my own gradual transformation back to aliveness. They let me know when I was slipping into burnout, and they applauded little breakthroughs into presence. Most of all, they celebrated me as a whole and valuable human being, regardless of where I was on the 12-stage burnout continuum at any given moment. It was authenticity that mattered the most to them.

The day before I turned in the manuscript, FBF and real-life friend Oriah House (also known as Oriah Mountain Dreamer) posted the following:

> Joanie, I just opened FB and there you are, on at the same time. Yes indeed, we teach what we need to learn, because (hopefully) our struggle with what we write/teach about can offer something to others. We don't ask someone who is a natural at something to teach us how to do it—he or she won't be able to articulate it because it comes *naturally*. The best teachers are the ones who continue to have to consciously practice what they teach.

What I'm practicing is so simple that it's really easy to miss. Burnout disappears in the Now because there's no separation between you and life unfolding. You are present and accounted for, immersed in a harmonious dance with the moment. This is love in its bare-bones state, a deep connection and appreciation that opens the door to eternity. And in that timeless state, you can sometimes see forever—or at least as far as the next horizon. Step after elegant step, you can follow your bliss into the fullest expression of life flowing through your own authentic, unique self.

The Power of Presence

In these times of change, corporations, like individuals, are increasingly interested in how they can tune in to what Otto Scharmer, senior lecturer at MIT, calls "the future that wants to emerge." Divining the future used to be the province of fortune-tellers rather than consultants for Fortune 500 companies. Scharmer works with international institutions and governments and has co-designed award-winning business leadership programs for world-renowned client firms, focusing on "building people's collective capacity to achieve profound innovation and change."[1]

To that end, Scharmer formed the Presencing Institute, and the word *presencing* is defined as "a journey that connects us more deeply both to what wants to emerge in the world and to our emerging, originating self."[2]

I love that—the recognition by a business consultant and visionary that our highest future possibility (what I call heaven on Earth) is the emergence of our authentic self as it peeks out in moments of presence.

FBF Len Delony described presence as being "open in gratitude in a way that opens the eyes and ears of the heart." This, he continued, helps us become open to our vocation—our personal future that wants to emerge. Len added this to the discussion:

> Wow! This conversation on burnout sure struck a chord with a lot of people! I've been following that question for at least 15 years in a "healing community" as a hospital chaplain, more recently as a spiritual director connected with a Methodist church. I agree that it seems

to be more about heart than busyness. However, without ongoing contemplative rhythms (broadly defined), it is often too hard to connect with and be present to our deepest desires and callings.

Our culture generally focuses too quickly on goals and productivity, often at an addictive pace. Everyone is unique in how vocation unfolds, but a common question is, "What helps me be open in gratitude, and attentive in a way that opens the eyes and ears of the heart?" With a heartfelt sense of vocation, work seems more passionately creative and sustainable. But how can we find better balance for our work and unhurried rhythms for simple, gracious presence in our living?

The FBFs shared their own ways of finding the contemplative rhythm and balance that leads to mindful presence in the Now. I know from personal experience that identifying a practice that works for you and sticking with it *religiously* is a prerequisite for reigniting your passion and connecting with the Spirit of Guidance.

My own daily practice includes the natural meditation of breath, body awareness, and movement throughout the day; the enjoyment of nature; and loving—really seeing and relating to—Gordie, my friends, and my family members (both two- and four-legged). This simple, organic practice helps me feel less carried away by our fast-paced culture.

"The speed of life has increased," posted FBF Kamila Susan Harkavy, "but it's the speed of business that seems to be ever increasing. My ego responds to it and is stimulated by it, urging me to keep up with the Joneses. However, my spirit just can't accommodate it, so I take life at a pace that works for *me*. I allow as much time as I need for contemplative activities, I practice yoga, and I exercise outdoors."

FBF Thapkay Dolkar shared the following:

> A walk in nature is always full of inspiration for me. It combines physical, mental, and emotional presence into a total experience. It's much more than a sensory experience. If I tap into a poetic or intuitive expression of myself, this is definitely rejuvenating—letting go while remaining grounded to the present.

FBF Christine Hibbard echoed the healing power of nature, embodying the poetry that Thapkay Dolkar mentioned:

> The body knows when to restore itself . . . resting in silence, glorious, clear blue sky, abundant fields of wildflowers. . . . We shed our old form, and the butterfly spreads its wings.

FBF Jim Rheinhardt has a unique way of fanning his inner flame:

> When I'm feeling a lack of enthusiasm, Divine inspiration is always the key for me to a return to a higher energy level. Some people get that from walks in nature or meditation. And although I love both of those methods, I find

that engaging my perceived problems head-on with love and gratitude results in Divine inspiration and increased enthusiasm.

What struck me most about the Facebook conversations on presence were the unique responses of each person. Our individual differences in how and why we burn out and the ways in which we revive and rekindle our enthusiasm for life reflects our *authenticity,* which is the subject of our final chapter. As we plunged deep into the Burnout Inferno and reflected inwardly while traveling through purgatory, we've finally reached heaven on Earth. Welcome to paradise!

Chapter Eight

Heaven on Earth

"The dream you are living is your creation. It is your perception of reality that you can change at any time. You have the power to create hell, and you have the power to create heaven. Why not dream a different dream? Why not use your mind, your imagination, and your emotions to dream heaven?"

— FROM *THE FOUR AGREEMENTS*, BY DON MIGUEL RUIZ

We began our journey exploring the mysteries of burnout. Our first stop was the *Inferno,* the lonely abode of fried souls. We examined the 12 stages of burnout and engaged in self-reflective exercises that showed us how to start moving beyond them. We delved deeply into why some of us give up hope more easily than others, which childhood and adult factors relate to depression, and the role of our temperament in burnout. Finally, we examined ways to manage our energy and achieve balance so that we could feel alive and vital in the present moment.

For most of the journey, we've been in the equivalent of Dante's *Purgatorio,* that cosmic treatment center where recovery begins. Dante described it thusly. (Did I really just write *thusly?* Whatever.) This is what he wrote:

> *And of that second kingdom will I sing*
> *Wherein the human spirit doth purge itself,*
> *And to ascend to heaven becometh worthy.*[1]

Awakened to our less-than-stellar patterns of burned-out thoughts and behaviors, and purged of the desire to create more suffering for ourselves, we are now ready to graduate to the third stop on our hero's journey: *Paradiso*.

Remember that *The Divine Comedy* moves from the earth down to hell, through purgatory, and then rises up to paradise. Its shape is a smile. The joke, of course, is on us. The entire journey through the circles of hell (in our case, the 12 stages of burnout) happens inside our own minds. As the English poet John Milton wrote some 300 years after Dante's death (in his epic poem *Paradise Lost*): "The mind is its own place, and in itself / Can make Heaven of Hell, a Hell of Heaven."

Just as children exist naturally in a state of heaven, so can we as adults. We just have to live in the soul by being who we are—our authentic selves. That doesn't sound difficult, but actually living from the core self, the natural mind, is an art—one that burning out can awaken us to.

My colleague and friend Lee McCormick, a long-time student of Don Miguel Ruiz and a shaman in his own right, operates a recovery center called The Ranch in Nunnelly, Tennessee. (He is also the co-owner of The Dreaming House near Teotihuacán, Mexico, where guests can go on sacred journeys to reconnect with their authentic selves.) Lee wrote the following on living an authentic life:

Being authentic is the natural condition of humans. When we are authentic, we express spontaneously with love and joy for life. As young children we started out connected to Nature, to Spirit, to the wholeness of Life, and felt free to express that connection. As we grew, we began to be programmed in order to fit into society's beliefs. Some of these beliefs served us well, and many created conflict within ourselves. We learned to modify our behavior, to emulate what we thought we were supposed to be and not what we really were. We started self-judging and self-rejecting based on what we were taught, and as a result, we lost our authentic selves.[2]

Revival from burnout is always about the recovery of lost authenticity. It's waking up to who we really are and realizing that heaven is not a destination, but a state of mind. If being fried can bring us to the point where we reconnect to our own true nature, then it's worth every moment of separation to rediscover the heaven that has been inside of us all along.

In one of our early virtual salons, FBF Peter Bolland wrote about burnout as "a necessary wintertime of pulling back, drawing down, and eventual renewal . . . a tremendously positive course correction. It could be the soul's attempt to communicate something to the mind." I like the idea of burnout being part of a natural cycle—a mysterious inner-guidance system that keeps us on track.

As I sit here at my desk this final morning of writing, I'm rereading some of the conversations that the FBFs and I have had about burnout over this past year. I take a deep breath and another sip of tea. I'm happy. It's summer now: the snow has melted, wildflowers have sprouted from the mud . . . the long winter has finally passed, literally and figuratively. It's a good time to reflect on the journey:

> *There's a time and a season for everything. A time for exhaustion and a time for rest. A time for doing and a time for being. A time for being burned out and a time to appreciate what burnout has taught us. Learning to recognize its early signs has been a big help for me. When I catch myself pushing, even though I'm exhausted, I stop and rest. Instead of running after my own agenda, I wait for Life's invitation.*

Here are more final thoughts from some of the FBFs:

> *LeeAnn Gibbs:* Every time I've hit the burnout wall, it's because I've refused to follow that voice inside that says it's time for a new adventure. I have held on so tightly to what I think has been my good, I've been afraid that there isn't something better . . . and there always is.

> *Christina J. Del Piero:* My body seems to hold a particular wisdom. I find that if I pay attention to physical symptoms and sensations with a meditative openness, trying to comprehend

my body's "secret language"—the way that one might pay attention to a preverbal child or beloved animal—I am often led to expansive, new perceptions. A regular hatha yoga practice brings surprising joy and helps sensitize me to the language of my body; reducing physical constriction seems to generate emotional and spiritual expansion.

Slim Chandra-Shekar: The Universe is a reflection of our attitude toward it. If we have a pessimistic nature and approach to life, the Universe will appear dark and unfriendly to us. If we are openhearted and see life and the human experience with friendly, loving eyes and have a positive attitude, the Universe will appear friendly, and we will see the gifts it offers.

Alan Sunbeam: If you consider the "old dream" to be an old habit, then you can consider the "new dream" to be a new habit. How does one move out of an old habit and into a new one? By noticing when the old habit is happening and consciously moving to the new habit consistently and as often as necessary until the new habit is established.

Melissa Epple: How do you create heaven on Earth? By doing just what you did, Joan. Ask a provocative and challenging question, and the part of the brain that functions creatively gets triggered. Do this with small teams of three people and watch them become energized.

I work in a school district that is dealing with layoffs and recently facilitated a teacher session. People came in very depressed and feeling victimized. However, after utilizing a simple protocol allowing them to reflect upon, write about, and share "what they did in this past year in a teaming situation to achieve something extraordinary, and who will they be when they go to a job interview," they left feeling enthusiastic and efficacious.

Amanda Bridget Griffin: Burnout usually begins long before we hit the edge. Someone long ago used to say to me, "When you come to the end of your rope, tie a knot in it and start climbing." I believed that until my hands could no longer remember how to tie a knot.

To prevent burnout, listen to yourself, rest when you need to, and love your body in the way you eat and what your senses take in . . . spend time in silence, do yoga, meditate, take walks in nature. Talk or write, but don't let anything fester.

Learn to breathe. Getting in touch with your breath and being conscious of your life force can change everything. Find joy in simple things. To restore yourself from burnout, the same applies: unplug for a few hours or days—the world won't stop turning without all your doing! But if you don't stop and take care of yourself, *you* might stop turning. Meditate on things to be grateful for, even if it's only one small thing—it will grow in your awareness. Be good to yourself, put yourself first, and love yourself so that when you are strong enough, you can give to others. Blessings, and thanks, Joan, for giving us this space to share.

Blessings and thanks to *you* my friends—old and new—for showing up and joining the conversation. And if you're not already a member of our virtual community on Facebook, please come and join us at **www .facebook.com/pages/Boulder-CO/Joan-Borysenko/ 211406562428.**

Your Epitaph

My good friend, humorist and author Loretta La-Roche, teaches ways to enjoy the present moment and live a "juicy life." To gain direction and stay focused, she recommends writing your own eulogy and epitaph. Thinking about how others will remember you when you're gone can be powerful motivation to make positive changes today.

To keep your attention (and true to Loretta's style), she came up with several quirky epitaphs known as the "Tombstone No One Wants." My favorite one, which has helped me turn off the computer and go for a walk on many a day, is: GOT IT ALL DONE. DEAD ANYWAY.

Carpe diem. Enjoy life while you can, because in spite of all its ordeals and challenges, it's over much too soon. You will never regret the days you spent walking in the fields, working in the garden, playing with your animal companions, and loving your family and friends. In all the years I've listened to dying people share the wisdom from their lives, not once did anyone wish they had spent more time working.

Let your "doing" arise organically from being in the Now. You will get much more done—and with an unparalleled elegance and creative genius—when your work grows from the inspiration that flows through you rather than from the effort of squeezing your own adrenals.

Do whatever it takes to appreciate the wonder of the unique expression of Life that you are. When you can do that, you will live in heaven on Earth.

Endnotes

Preface

1. *The Divine Comedy of Dante Alighieri,* translated by Henry Wadsworth Longfellow (*Inferno,* Canto I).

Chapter 1

1. FBF Jan Carmichael Davies, who offered this comment, is a hospice volunteer and whole health educator.

2. Herbert J. Freudenberger, with Geraldine Richelson, *Burnout: The High Cost of High Achievement.* Garden City, NY: Anchor Press, 1980.

3. The "stages of burnout" list cited by Carmen Pickering in *The Stress of Work or the Work of Stress, Health, and Learning* (Promoting Healthy Lifestyles, Canadian Teachers' Federation, Winter 2008) was adapted from Ulrich Kraft, "Burned Out: Your job is extremely fulfilling. It is also extremely demanding—and you feel overwhelmed. You are not alone." *Scientific American Mind,* June/July 2006, pp. 29–33.

4. Thomas Merton, "Letter to a Young Activist": **http://bintana.tripod.com/ref/letter.htm**.

5. Ibid.

6. S.S. Chopra, W.M. Sotile, and M.O. Sotile, "Physician Burnout," *JAMA,* 2004, p. 291: 633.

7. V. Brenninkmeijer, N.W. Van Yperen, and B.P. Buunk, "Burnout and Depression Are Not Identical Twins: Is Superiority a Distinguishing Feature?" *Personality and Individual Differences,* vol. 30, April 2001, pp. 873–880.

Chapter 2

1. The author of this quote is unknown, but it appeared in *The American Legion Magazine* as cited by: **http://blog .gaiam.com/quotes/authors/unknown/37413**.

2. This heading was inspired by David Healy's book *Let Them Eat Prozac: The Unhealthy Relationship Between the Pharmaceutical Industry and Depression.* (New York: New York University Press, 2004).

3. Carl Elliott, "The Drug Pushers," *The Atlantic,* April 2006: **www.theatlantic.com/doc/200604/drug-reps**.

4. SSRI Withdrawal Support Site: **http://ssri-uksupport .com/files/homicidesSSRISandADHDmedications.pdf**.

5. Ibid.

6. Christopher Bollyn, "America Over-Dosed: The Role of Anti-Depressants in the Columbine Tragedy & Other Bizarre Killings," *American Free Press,* June 2006.

7. For a good summary of more recent studies on the statistical correlation between depression and suicide, go to: **http://mentalhealth.samhsa.gov/ suicideprevention/risks.asp**.

8. Irving Kirsch et al., "Initial Severity and Antidepressant Benefits: A Meta-Analysis of Data Submitted to the Food and Drug Administration," 2008:

www.plosmedicine.org/article/info:doi/10.1371/
journal.pmed.0050045.

9. NACBT Online Headquarters: www.nacbt.org/
whatiscbt.htm.

Chapter 3

1. Vincent J. Felitti, "The Relationship of Adverse
Childhood Experiences in Adult Health: Turning Gold
into Lead," *The Permanente Journal,* vol. 6, no. 1, Winter
2002.

2. Ibid.

3. Ibid.

Chapter 4

1. To learn more about the benefits of increasing your stress
hardiness, visit The Hardiness Institute, Inc.: www
.hardinessinstitute.com/Personal.htm.

2. For an overview of David Keirsey's Four Temperaments,
go to: www.keirsey.com/handler.aspx?s=keirsey&f=
fourtemps&tab=3&c=overview.

3. www.keirsey.com/handler.aspx?s=keirsey&f=fourtemps
&tab=3&c=teacher.

Chapter 5

1. The diagram of the Tree of Life can be found on
Wikipedia: http://en.wikipedia.org/wiki/Sephirot.

2. Rabbi Shimon Leiberman, "Tiferet: Beautiful Synthesis," July 2000: **www.aish.com/sp/k/48965381.html**.

Chapter 7

1. Otto Scharmer: **www.ottoscharmer.com/bio**.

2. Presencing Institute: **www.presencinginstitute.com**.

Chapter 8

1. *The Divine Comedy of Dante Alighieri,* translated by Henry Wadsworth Longfellow (*Purgatorio,* Canto I).

2. Lee McCormick, "Spirit Recovery": **www.spiritrecovery .com**. The Ranch Website is at: **www.recoveryranch .com**.

Acknowledgments

First and foremost, thank you to my Facebook friends whose engagement in a yearlong conversation about burnout and revival brought both me and this book to life.

Some of them wandered in and out of the conversation, leaving an occasional jewel in their wake. Others were a more constant presence, frequently posting wisdom and wisecracks, photos and videos. Even more held the space behind the scenes. When our beautiful canine companion Skye, a two-year-old standard poodle, suddenly took sick and died six weeks before this manuscript was due, the Facebook community showed up in force. The hundreds of messages of love and comfort that kept coming for weeks on FB, e-mail, and snail mail helped Gordon and me through one of life's more difficult passages.

David Jon Peckinpaugh is one of my most treasured FBFs. When I looked up one of his books (*Buddha & Shakespeare: Eastern Dharma, Western Drama*) on Amazon, the About the Author section resonated with my experience of him: "Inspired by the works of such American luminaries as Ralph Waldo Emerson and Henry David Thoreau, David Jon Peckinpaugh continues to seek a return of the many blessings that he himself has received from the hands and hearts of others, by adding his voice to the symphony of a distinctly American brand of philosophy and discourse." When he wrote that description of himself, he may not have been thinking of Facebook as a brand of philosophy and discourse. But it can be, and certainly is, in David's blogs and postings.

When it came time to name this book, David was the one who came up with the title, remarking, "I wonder if the word *Fried* happens to catch this moment, Joan: that there is this cultural milieu we are all immersed in—where so much information is coming at us, to the point that many of us feel overwhelmed by it . . . like we're about to blow a circuit or two!"

The final title decision was a three-day marathon that many of the FBFs participated in. It was so much fun—and so addictive—that it was hard to leave the computer. *Fried* went head-to-head with *Hell Is a Bad Place to Pitch a Tent* from FBF Richard Held. Thank you so much, Richard. Your fine line is immortalized in the Preface.

Many thanks to psychologist and author Beverly Potter, my virtual fairy godmother. Her tremendous generosity of spirit and willingness to share extensive knowledge about burnout got me off to a great start. That anyone would be so kind to a stranger is a testimony to who she is. In addition to posting in the public conversations, Beverly and I maintained a rich private conversation, also on FB, that spurred me on and helped me realize that I had something new to offer in this book.

Deb Somfay, Maria Petrova, Slim Chandra-Shekar, Denise Linn, Vickie Byard, Doris Goodill, Theresa Da-Kay, Margaret Lewis, Janise Rennie, Constance McClain, Thapkay Dolkar, Edie Weinstein, Lori Landau, Chuck E. Davis, Lauren Rosenfeld, Michele Lawson, Marilyn Joyce, Bonita Yoder, Oriah House, Steve Frazee, Toni

Venz, Mary-Lynne Monroe, Keith Bell (my YaYa Boi) . . . are just a *few* of the loyal Facebook gang I want to thank for their wisdom and their love. There were so many wonderful postings about burnout and revival that there wasn't enough room to include them all. They are in the book nonetheless, speaking from between the lines.

My colleague and friend Lee McCormick—shaman, rascal, and wise man—thanks for taking Gordon and me to Teotihuacán, introducing us to the work of Don Miguel Ruiz, and giving us a memorable experience of deconstructing our place in hell and moving on to find heaven on Earth. You're an inspiration to me and to the entire field of recovery and mental health. And thanks, too, to Maru Ahumada. You brought Don Miguel's teachings to life in my heart.

My husband, colleague, and best friend, Gordon Dveirin, knows about my penchant for burning out firsthand. He's swept up the ashes more times than I'd like to admit, always with gracious love and patience. To live with a person who sees and encourages you— with clarity but never criticism—is a gift I would wish for everyone. Gordie knows what it's like for me to write a book, since we've written two together (*Saying Yes to Change* and *Your Soul's Compass*). Now that *Fried* is done, it's time to pull out the cowboy boots and go dancing at the Grizzly Rose, darlin'!

Chris and David Hibbard—as always, your heartfelt support, meaningful conversation, great hospitality, and occasional road trips to get away from it all helped me through the writing process. Sarah Davidson, my friend and a truly great writer, thank you for your love and encouragement. Karen Drucker, Cheryl Richardson, Debbie Ford, Robin Casarjian, Luzie and Bob Mason, Justin and Regina Borysenko, Andrei and Nadia Borysenko—thank you all for your support, insight, and love. And as always, a big thanks to my Hay House family: the inimitable Louise Hay, who was one of my first teachers; Reid Tracy, my publisher and friend who has let me speak my "peace" for 20 years; editorial director and brainstorming partner Jill Kramer; my fabulous editor Lisa Mitchell, who worked magic with the text; Christy Salinas, who designed the cover; Jami Goddess, who designed the interior; my publicist Richelle Zizian; Webmaster for **HealYourLife.com** Donna Abate; and all the people behind the scenes who make Hay House such a force for good in the world.

About the Author

Joan Borysenko, Ph.D., is a Harvard-trained medical scientist, licensed psychologist, and spiritual educator. A *New York Times* best-selling author and blogger for The Huffington Post, her work has appeared in newspapers ranging from *The Washington Post* to *The Wall Street Journal*. A warm and engaging teacher and speaker, she blends cutting-edge science and psychology with a profound and palpable sense of the sacred (and a world-class sense of humor). Founder and director of the Soul-Care in HealthCare training program, her vision is to remind us all that the relationship is the medicine.

Joan lives in the mountains of Colorado with her husband, Gordon Dveirin, and their two dogs, Sophie and Milo. You can find out more about her work, watch videos, and read articles at **www.joanborysenko.com**. You are also welcome to join the lively conversation on Joan's Facebook page at: **www.facebook.com/pages/Boulder-CO/Joan-Borysenko/211406562428**.

Hay House Titles of Related Interest

YOU CAN HEAL YOUR LIFE, the movie,
starring Louise L. Hay & Friends
(available as a 1-DVD program and an expanded 2-DVD set)
Watch the trailer at: **www.LouiseHayMovie.com**

THE SHIFT, the movie,
starring Dr. Wayne W. Dyer
(available as a 1-DVD program and an expanded 2-DVD set)
Watch the trailer at: **www.DyerMovie.com**

~~O~~

The Art of Extreme Self-Care: *Transform Your
Life One Month at a Time,* by Cheryl Richardson

Experience Your Good Now!
Learning to Use Affirmations, by Louise L. Hay

The Four Agreements, by Don Miguel Ruiz (a 48-card deck)

Inspiration Deficit Disorder: *The No-Pill
Prescription to End High Stress, Low Energy,
and Bad Habits,* by Jonathan H. Ellerby, Ph.D.

Relax—You May Only Have a Few Minutes Left:
Using the Power of Humor to Overcome Stress in Your Life and Work,
by Loretta LaRoche

This Is the Moment! *How One Man's
Yearlong Journey Captured the Power of
Extraordinary Gratitude,* by Walter Green

Unlock the Secret Messages of Your Body!
*A 28-Day Jump-Start Program for Radiant Health
and Glorious Vitality,* by Denise Linn

All of the above are available at your local bookstore,
or may be ordered by contacting Hay House (see next page).

~~O~~

We hope you enjoyed this Hay House book. If you'd like to receive our online catalog featuring additional information on Hay House books and products, or if you'd like to find out more about the Hay Foundation, please contact:

HAY HOUSE

Hay House, Inc., P.O. Box 5100, Carlsbad, CA 92018-5100
(760) 431-7695 or (800) 654-5126
(760) 431-6948 (fax) or (800) 650-5115 (fax)
www.hayhouse.com® • **www.hayfoundation.org**

Published and distributed in Australia by:
Hay House Australia Pty. Ltd., 18/36 Ralph St.,
Alexandria NSW 2015 • *Phone:* 612-9669-4299
Fax: 612-9669-4144 • www.hayhouse.com.au

Published and distributed in the United Kingdom by:
Hay House UK, Ltd., 292B Kensal Rd., London W10 5BE
Phone: 44-20-8962-1230 • *Fax:* 44-20-8962-1239
www.hayhouse.co.uk

Published and distributed in the Republic of South Africa by:
Hay House SA (Pty), Ltd., P.O. Box 990, Witkoppen 2068
Phone/Fax: 27-11-467-8904 • www.hayhouse.co.za

Published in India by: Hay House Publishers India, Muskaan
Complex, Plot No. 3, B-2, Vasant Kunj, New Delhi 110 070
Phone: 91-11-4176-1620 • *Fax:* 91-11-4176-1630
www.hayhouse.co.in

Distributed in Canada by: Raincoast, 9050 Shaughnessy St.,
Vancouver, B.C. V6P 6E5 • *Phone:* (604) 323-7100
Fax: (604) 323-2600 • www.raincoast.com

Take Your Soul on a Vacation

Visit **www.HealYourLife.com®** to regroup, recharge,
and reconnect with your own magnificence.
Featuring blogs, mind-body-spirit news, and life-changing
wisdom from Louise Hay and friends.

Visit **www.HealYourLife.com** today!

Heal Your Life One Thought at a Time . . .
on Louise's All-New Website!

*"Life is bringing me everything
I need and more."*

— Louise Hay

Come to HEALYOURLIFE.COM today and meet the world's best-selling self-help authors; the most popular leading intuitive, health, and success experts; up-and-coming inspirational writers; and new like-minded friends who will share their insights, experiences, personal stories, and wisdom so you can heal your life and the world around you . . . one thought at a time.

Here are just some of the things you'll get at HealYourLife.com:

- DAILY AFFIRMATIONS
- CAPTIVATING VIDEO CLIPS
- EXCLUSIVE BOOK REVIEWS
- AUTHOR BLOGS
- LIVE TWITTER AND FACEBOOK FEEDS
- BEHIND-THE-SCENES SCOOPS
- LIVE STREAMING RADIO
- "MY LIFE" COMMUNITY OF FRIENDS

PLUS:
FREE Monthly Contests and Polls
FREE BONUS gifts, discounts,
and newsletters

Make It Your Home Page Today!
www.HealYourLife.com®

HEAL YOUR LIFE®♥